∞

*Please Don't Drink
the Holy Water!*

Susie Lloyd

Please Don't Drink the Holy Water!

Homeschool Days, Rosary Nights,
and Other Near Occasions of Sin

SOPHIA INSTITUTE PRESS®
Manchester, New Hampshire

Sophia Institute Press®
Box 5284, Manchester, NH 03108
1-800-888-9344
www.sophiainstitute.com

Library of Congress Cataloging-in-Publication Data

Lloyd, Susie, 1966-
    Please don't drink the holy water! : homeschool days, rosary nights, and other near occasions of sin / Susie Lloyd.
        p. cm.
    ISBN 1-928832-19-9 (pbk. : alk. paper)
    1. Home schooling — Humor. 2. Catholics — Humor.
I. Title: Please do not drink the holy water!. II. Title.

PN6231.H56L66 2004
814'.6 — dc22   2004021520

04 05 06 07 08 09 10 9 8 7 6 5 4 3 2 1

*To Greg and my five girlfriends,
a measure pressed down and running over.
Together with the Author of the Real World,
they made me a mother.*

*And special thanks to Elizabeth,
my Real World writer buddy.*

∞

Contents

Introduction

Part 1
Moms, Don't Try
This at Home

Part 2
Driving Under the
Influence of Guilt

Part 3
Trust Providence —
Not to Warn You What's Coming

Part 4

Just Between You and Me
and the Crayon on the Walls

Biographical Note

∞

Will the "Real World" Please Stand Up?

"How are your kids going to make it in the Real World?"

Do you get that question a lot? If so, you must be a Catholic parent — maybe even that strange and mysterious subspecies: a homeschooler.

You hear it at parties and supermarkets, at the doctor's and the grocer's. It comes in tones of curiosity, concern, or thinly disguised skepticism. It can make you pause and stammer — not out of embarrassment, but simply because you're unsure of how to answer.

That's because it's one of those questions that don't really have an answer. In fact, it isn't even a real question. As a teaching parent, I'd give it an Incomplete.

What, after all, is the Real World? *Where* is the Real World?

When you start probing, you find out that the experts do have some clues:

It's big.

The only chance your kids have is to hand them over to experts — that is, anybody but yourself — because as a parent you are inclined to shelter them from it, and we wouldn't want that.

It's elite.

Its inhabitants belong to an exclusive club that churns out conventional wisdom. Members are known as "they," as in the phrase, "They say . . ."

A great divide separates us from them.

Catholics who take seriously the admonition to be *in* the world but not *of* it are living in a dangerous place called Shelterhaven. We cannot cross over from our side to theirs.

It's a nice place to live, but you wouldn't want to visit.

Any child brought up in Shelterhaven would immediately die of shock in the Real World. Therefore, parents should send their kids into it as soon as possible, especially if they show unhealthy signs, like getting too attached to their mother in preschool.

The Real World. It's one of those catch phrases designed to strike parents dumb with fear. It looms ahead like a black hole. It's unfamiliar, it's big, it's "out there." It's waiting to suck us in!

But fear not. In fact, the Real World is familiar, manageable, and sitting around your kitchen table. It's the Catholic family on the road to heaven.

The Lloyd family has been homeschooling right from the beginning. Our oldest is now a teenager. I've written tens of thousands of words on the subject, from prayers that are guaranteed to keep your kid out of hell to where to buy a cow's eyeball.

This book is about the very Real World of a Catholic family, just trying to do the best we can. We're every bit a part of the twenty-first century even if we are down in the catacombs attempting to live by first-century values. Sometimes a bit of pagan Rome creeps in, yet we keep trying in the very real hope that we may laugh at all of it someday with the first Christians in the *real* Real World.

∞

Please Don't Drink
the Holy Water!

Part 1

Moms, Don't Try
This at Home

∞

Keeping Up Appearances

For a second, I thought I was on *Candid Camera*. There we were, the six of us, on a weekday in early afternoon, dutifully finishing up our schoolwork while maxing out the chairs in our ophthalmologist's narrow waiting room.

A seasoned gentleman who had been openly watching us for a half-hour finally spoke. "Where do you go to school?" he asked our third daughter. An able man, I marveled. Four out of five kids with the gift of language, and he zeroes in on the reporter among them.

One glance told me he must be a retired professional. A grandfatherly type. Good with kids. There was a definite twinkle in his eye. Safe.

I nodded at Miss Three. "We're homeschoolers," she began.

The guy turned out to be Barbara Walters in disguise.

"Really? Do you like it?

"How many hours a day do you spend at it?

"Do you have social activities?

"Do you have a blackboard?

"Do you have a computer?

"Oh, two computers, but no blackboard? Hmmm. . . ."

Before Miss Three invited him over for a tour of our kitchen table, I felt it was time to step in.

Truth is, I was waiting for an opening anyway. I welcome a chance to put a good face on homeschooling — show a member of the "greatest generation" just how responsible and by-the-book we homeschoolers can be.

I paused before beginning. Should I quote statistics showing off our academic savvy? Or maybe I should hit the social angle. Perhaps he had already noticed how well-behaved and articulate my children were.

"You see . . ." I began, lifting my chin slightly.

Suddenly Miss Firstborn slammed down her English workbook. "I can't do it! I just can't do it!" she shrieked. "I just don't *get* it! What's the point of learning this stuff anyway? When I grow up, no one's ever going to ask me what an appositive is — I guarantee it! If I die young, I'll never even *use* it!"

I glanced furtively at the fellow. He hadn't flinched. With a look, I nailed my daughter to her chair and tried to reassemble my speech.

He beat me to it. "I taught public school for many years," he said.

"Oh?" I said, smiling tolerantly.

"That is, until I became principal."

"Really?"

"Yes. Then I was superintendent for some years before I retired."

"Well, well . . ."

"I find it very interesting that you are homeschooling," he continued, smiling tolerantly. "Do you mind if I ask you a question?"

I looked down at the floor and shrugged.

"I was only wondering how you plan to manage neurochemical gross anatomy and other such advanced subjects when these children get to high school."

Just then, the receptionist entered — "Mrs. Lloyd?"

Deus ex machina, right on cue. I could have hugged her. In fact, at that moment I could have given her my firstborn. But as I rose to go, I remembered my duty. I am a homeschooler. I am pioneer stock. I AM WOMAN! I raised myself to my full five-foot-three, faced the school superintendent, and pronounced, "I plan to drive off that bridge when I get to it."

Then an amazing thing happened. He laughed. In his eyes there was a definite twinkle.

After years of homeschooling, my moment had come. Face-to-face with a bonafide educational expert, and I didn't even have to use my speech.

I looked around for Allen Funt to jump out, point to the hidden camera, and tell me what I'd won. But I saw no one.

It had to be the Holy Ghost.

∞

Sorry, My Brain Is Spoken For

My poor husband. When we got married, he thought he was getting an intellectual partner. He was finishing a Master's in philosophy; I had just graduated from a liberal-arts college with a philosophy major. He and I used to spend hours discussing lofty things like the Ontological Argument and Intersubjective Verifiability. The only breaks in these discussions came when his mother would walk through the room exclaiming, "Who the #%&* cares?!"

We used to take it as comic relief, but now I'm beginning to see her point.

Not that lofty things don't matter. It's just that I've learned to trust that metaphysical realities like the existence of God can get along without my help.

Cleaning the bathroom, however, can't.

Yes, by necessity I've traded the sublime for the ridiculous — on every day but Sunday, which is the Catholic day off. (God — *and I do trust You're out there* — is good.) It's not just the household chores that occupy my mind. Nor is it only the care and feeding of the multitude. The one thing that has most stymied my intellectual career is homeschooling.

Please Don't Drink the Holy Water!

Before I go on, let me say that I am not what I'd call a dummy. (Then again, not many people think of themselves as dummies. Hence, the question arises, do dummies really know they're dummies? To which the answer is: Who the #%&?* cares?!) To add to this concept of not being a dummy, let me also say that after ten years of homeschooling, I know enough *facts* about everything (except maybe pop culture) to go on *Jeopardy.* I'm so well versed in English grammar that I bore myself. Math, which in the past always shunned me, is now my bosom friend. In short, everything from ninth grade (my oldest child) down is my area of expertise. In addition, I have streamlined the process of diversification through the Command and Delegate functions (translation: I run everybody's lives and tell them what to do) so effectively that I am probably qualified to run a small corporation. Or at least talk as if I can.

Then there is keeping up with state standards — which requires a pile of paperwork documenting educational goals and progress, evaluation by a certified teacher, standardized testing, immunizations, height, weight, hearing, vision, physicals, dental exams, accepted diploma and transcript programs, and probably more if the Pennsylvania Department of Education weren't as sick of it as I am.

Did I mention I'm learning algebra?

My husband, on the other hand, is engaged in creative intellectual pursuits all day long at his job running a Catholic non-profit organization. And after a long day of pursuing creative intellectuals, he comes home geared up for more. Back in graduate school, his friends used to say no one had more philosophical stamina than Greg. After a two-hour class, he used to stay and conduct the "afterclass" — another two hours. Time, age, and worldly cares have not changed him. Greg's mode of relaxation is to read magazines that contain exclusive interviews with hierarchs from patriarchates who analyze Vatican decisions in light of history, theology, and ecclesiology. If you combine this with the fact that, through genetics and conditioning, he's a natural salesman, you get someone who never quits bringing home books and articles that I have absolutely no use for.

This isn't to say that these aren't worthy products. His latest, a four-hundred-page work entitled *Eastern Monastic Psychotherapy* is undoubtedly the result of much prayer and study. However, right now the most stimulating reading I can handle is the back of a cereal box.

I am a homeschooler. My brain is spoken for.

Then there are books suggested by educated people who have read my magazine articles. Somehow they've gotten the impression

"Don't disturb Mom. She's catching up on her reading."

that I know something and are eager to make me even better informed by suggesting books like *Who's Who of Today's Closet Heretics* and *A Pictorial History of Demonic Possession Since Vatican II* (a coffee-table book). But due to overexposure in my younger days, I have developed an immunity to recreational reading of this sort.

My husband holds out hope that someday I will go back to being a libraphile. (That's "book lover" to you and me.) What he doesn't realize is that I still am — it's just that my affections have shifted. If you want to know, the books that really hold the key to my heart are workbooks. This is because, contrary to their name, the function of workbooks is to prevent work.

Workbooks, once held in lofty disdain by women who had only one kid to educate, are becoming a staple of home education. But that isn't the way I planned it.

When I started homeschooling, Miss Firstborn was four and a half. (I was too excited about homeschooling to wait for her to turn five.) It was just her and me and Chaucer — yes, I actually read her the Middle English. She progressed to Shakespeare by age seven and at age eleven played Portia in Shakespeare in the Park.

She was going to have the best classical education I could muster. In addition to the primary sources I had left over from my own liberal-arts education, I ordered vocabulary, spelling, grammar, *McGrim's Readers* (Protestant), *Faith & Friendly Readers* (Catholic), a math workbook, textbook, teacher's manual, manipulatives, and video, a science workbook, textbook, teacher's manual, and home chemistry kit, *The Babyblue Catechism*, *Bible Stories*, history, and *Great Saints of the Americas* Flash Cards. Friends were unloading *Art Classics for Tots* and *Origami for the Average Child Prodigy*, so I grabbed those too.

Then there were stimulating extracurricular activities: acting, piano lessons, chorus, sewing, Glue Club, highland hula dancing, and make-a-hundred-papier-maché-rocks.

All that was left was the collage. After all, kids have to have a little fun, too. I cut out leaves; Miss Firstborn helped glue. Later I secretly repositioned her efforts because the thing was too lopsided. A certain degree of lopsidedness is appropriate, though, so I fixed it just enough to make it look as if a small child had done it.

Day after day, Miss Firstborn sat there at the kitchen table and worked her heart out as her little sisters played around us. This was no kindergarten! This was serious!

Miss Number Five, on the other hand, is still crayoning the furniture. She will be allowed to develop normally, not only because I now realize what an uptight silly ass I was with poor Miss Firstborn, but because I've clean run out of energy. Luckily, workbooks — good old self-teaching hands-on reliable workbooks — practically grow on trees in Homeschool Land. Call them homeschool convenience food. All they ask of a parent is twenty seconds to read and interpret the directions. The handy-dandy answer key does the correcting for me and stands patiently by in case the students need a quick reference. All the while, I am ever-present and available to my children. If they want me, they know where to find me.

I'll be behind a wall of cereal boxes.

∽

How the Great Books Prepared Me for a
Rewarding Career Teaching Cave Lingo

Once when I complained that the kids were acting like hair shirts for home and classroom, my husband, a former college professor, reminded me that education would have no purpose if children didn't start out ignorant. He seemed to think that would be enough to keep me from strangling them.

The trouble with this line of reasoning is that it's typically male. It sounds logical, but it doesn't hold up in the real world, which, in our household, is six-sevenths feminine.

Greg gets his argument from Socrates, a male who spent all of his noteworthy moments with other males exclusively, expounding the Western Canon — which in his day consisted solely of two hunks of chiseled slate and a mound of dirt that kept getting erased when it rained.

In other words, Socrates had it easy (not counting the unfortunate hemlock incident). His students were volunteers who were being maintained by working wives and who never interrupted to go to the bathroom or ask when lunch was.

Modern men who try Socrates' ideas out on their homeschooling wives are forgetting that it got him killed.

Please Don't Drink the Holy Water!

One day, still trying to convince me that ignorance, while not bliss, is at least acceptable, Greg says, "Consider Plato's cave analogy. This is like the journey from childhood to adulthood. Our imaginations start in the cave, where all is darkness and confusion. We then notice the shadows on the wall. If we have a spark of creative curiosity, we follow the shadows until the images become sharper. At last we break free into the light of the great wide-open space that is Truth. As Catholics, we like to think of the ultimate Truth as partaking of an eternal banquet. Children need to be guided by those of us who have already tasted of wisdom's table."

He is speaking to someone who has taught cave lingo for the last four kids. After a morning of "Ayah, ae, ah, buh, cuh, suh, duh," I tell him all I want is to partake of the divine nectar and potato salad alone in front of a Bishop Sheen rerun.

He tries a different line. "Okay, then, think of Virgil and Dante. Without Virgil guiding him, Dante might have gotten lost wandering around in the outer circle. Without you, how will the little Dantettes reach their depths?"

"You mean the First Circle?"

"Ha, ha," he says as he steadily grows more patient. "Wrong choice of words. Obviously the path I speak of is one of ascent. . . . "

"Purgatory is the next stop after the Inferno," I interject, "which means according to your analogy that I'll be stranded. Virgil didn't make it to the Paradiso. He was pagan, and Dante was medieval. Back in those days, there was a sign on the pearly gates that read, 'Pagans, keep out. Universal salvation hasn't been invented yet.' "

Greg sighs, "Yes, I believe you'll get all of us to Purgatory." Finally, he has said something I can grab on to. Hope!

I tell Greg that Purgatory is starting to look good to me. At the rate the kids are wearing me out, I might go there soon.

"The other day, I spent a half-hour explaining the causes of the Civil War to the threesome in my history class. I started with the effects of European Protestantism on the founding of our country, the idea of institutionalized rebellion coming back to haunt the proponents of centralized government, and the ramifications of the outcome on all subsequent policies right down to *Roe v. Wade*. Miss Teen raised her hand and said, 'Does this count as religion class too? I want to cross it off.' "

Greg embraces me tenderly. "I'd rather have you teaching the little Dantettes than anyone else in the world."

"Did you have to say that?"

"I trust you," he says warmly.

"As if I don't have enough to feel guilty about."

"Guilt! Who's talking about guilt?"

"You are! You just don't care!"

Greg doesn't understand the turn our conversation has managed to take. This is because right from the beginning he has been laboring under the delusion that he is talking to another man. His eyes register "woman," but have failed to send the appropriate signals to his brain. Consequently his brain persists in offering male solutions to female emotions.

When the "You just don't care" line is delivered, Greg's brain automatically erases the solution software and begins to self-destruct: "How can you say that after I've been sitting here trying to tell you what a wonderful mother you are?!"

"I can say it, because it's true! If you did care, you'd quit that stupid job and stay home and teach your children! You'd be in the cave!"

"How would we eat?"

"I could work. I would love to be the one who gets dressed in the morning. I could do my hair more than once a week. Can't you just see me power-walking in sneakers to a quaint nearby café on my lunch break? I envy you — eating lunches that haven't been reheated with people whose table manners you don't have to correct."

"And just what would you do to support this family?"

He had me there, but that was no reason to give in.

I thought for a moment. Answers bleeped across my feminine forehead.

• I could tour the world lecturing on how all modern languages developed from the rudimentary sounds of: ayah, ae, buh, duh.

• I could write a book on creative ways to correct table manners without choking on your food, such as banging out Morse code on the table.

• I could join a focus group on the effects of feminine rhetoric on the male brain.

But I could see that none of that would move him. My frazzled wits had to concede that he had already won the debate. So I raised my hand and asked to go to the bathroom. "By the way," I added. "When's lunch?"

∞

The Real World, Stardate 17.20

Herb: (dig, dig) Jane, I think I've found something here.

Jane: (dig, dig) What?

Herb: (sweep, sweep) A skull. It looks like another supermater.

Jane: Give me that. You're right! Female . . . drove a minivan . . . wait — it may have been a full-size . . . wore denim skirts . . . survived almost entirely on cold leftovers and chocolate.

Herb: She's the nineteenth we've found this month. What kind of place was this?

Jane: Some kind of watering hole. How did that inscription you found last week go again?

Herb: If you print it, they will come.

Jane: Hmmm . . . that rules out a soccer field. My guess is we're excavating a library. Course, it just as easily could have been a workbook warehouse. There were dozens of them in the United States centuries ago. They say the *domus doctus* breed of supermater thrived on them.

Please Don't Drink the Holy Water!

Herb: *Domus doctus?* That's right. There *was* a certain breed of supermom who did home teaching. We were always taught that they were comparatively rare. Yet it seems we've stumbled right into a whole field of them. What do we know about them?

Jane: Surviving official statistics show that it was a highly advanced way of life, with members living in relative harmony and contributing to the world around them — going to college, getting good jobs, raising families, paying taxes, and so on. Yet there is other evidence that conflicts with that. Sources closest to the *domus doctus* supermater — letters from members of a club called, H.R.u.M.F. (Hairdressers, Relatives, *und* Malfunctioning Friends) paint a gloomy picture. They contain challenges to the *domus doctus* supermater like, "How are your kids going to make it in the Real World if they've never shared crayons with thirty other children in the classroom?"

Herb: Hmm . . . compelling. Do we know the answer?

Jane: Fortunately a few written exchanges still exist. We know of one that went, "If they can get along with their siblings on an everyday basis, they can get along with anybody."

Herb: Interesting. Whatever became of *domus doctus* supermater?

Jane: Scientists differ. Some say it was gradual devolution, but I've never cared for that theory.

Herb: Why?

Jane: For one thing, the *domus doctus* supermater was thriving and reproducing. She had anywhere from twice to five times the usual number of offspring for the era. In fact, all around her, the population was heading for zero replacement rate.

Herb: So, if anything, her kind would have eventually taken over the planet.

Jane: Exactly.

Herb: Then why did she disappear? Do you think she consumed resources too quickly?

Jane: No. There is strong evidence that as fast as *domus doctus* and her offspring could consume workbooks, more were being written. Besides, workbooks, while a staple, were not the only thing on the diet. There was a healthy supply of text-books, readers, spellers, videos, math manipulatives, flash cards, crafts, cow's eyeballs, dissectible frogs, and let's not forget original sources such as Chaucer, Shakespeare, and Aristotle. And that just covered first grade.

Herb: I had no idea *domus doctus* was so intellectually advanced.

Jane: Neither did she.

Herb: Huh?

Jane: That's where my theory comes in. *Domus doctus,* being of no more native stamina than other supermaters, eventually died out owing to a mass-induced overdose of these resources.

Herb: You mean they all tried to take them all at once?

Jane: Possibly. It would be in keeping with what we know of their general life habits.

Herb: What, for instance?

Please Don't Drink the Holy Water!

Jane: Running offspring to extracurricular activities for one. Passenger vans with thousands of miles on them have been discovered not far from here. These contain not only petrified french fries on the floor and car seats in the back, but workbooks with telltale titles like *Art Classics for Tots* and *Origami for the Average Child Prodigy*, not to mention scripts for plays, violin music, and sports equipment.

Herb: Wow! What caused such an overdose?

Jane: Guilt mainly. Evidence taken from letters to H.R.u.M.F. confirms that *domus doctus* took every precaution to make sure her offspring did not miss out on what offspring from other supermaters got. It's called Hokey Pokey Syndrome.

Herb: Why?

Jane: In former times, conventionally educated offspring played the Hokey Pokey and other classroom games. The object was to wear the kids out before quiet time. In the home-teaching environment, however, it backfired by wearing the mother out. Other symptoms of the syndrome were activities like gluing collages and drawing timelines and planning college for children as young as five.

Herb: Shouldering the burden of her child's entire academic and social formation really got to her, didn't it?

Jane: There is no doubt. Failure was not an option. Still, there are some scientists who insist that a catastrophic event could have caused the extinction all at once.

Herb: You mean like a giant meteor fell on them?

Jane: No, a giant curriculum box.

∞

History Meets Improv

One of the fringe benefits of homeschooling is that I have finally gotten a solid primary-school education.

I got through the first five grades on the art of Improv. My role model was the Artful Dodger. Clever, imaginative, unconventional, and a brilliant escape artist. This life of crime led to enormous holes in my primary-education fact file, such as the date of the War of 1812 and why *pi* is square instead of round.

One of my worst subjects was fifth-grade Social Studies.

As I recall, it looked something like History in that it started with cave men and progressed in linear fashion up to the present day. Even though this was Catholic school and our teacher was a nun, times had changed. No more telling history from a stale incarnational perspective that views the coming of Christ as the central point of history. The new and improved theme was: "All civilizations developed in an equally boring way." Facts about goods imported and exported appeared to be gobbled up by most of the class, but I daydreamed the entire year.

The climax of that year was a project. We were supposed to pick a country in South America, draw a map, and write an essay about it. We had a few weeks to get it ready. I had been daydreaming when the assignment was given, but the following weeks should have told me something was up.

One day our teacher went up and down the aisles pointing at people. One by one my classmates said things like, "Argentina," "Brazil," "Peru," and so on. An interesting game. I didn't know how to play, but it seemed that repeats were allowed, so when the teacher came to me, I said, "Brazil." She seemed satisfied. The next week we played it again, only this time my classmates gave answers like, "World Book Encyclopedia," "Encyclopedia Americana," and "Encyclopaedia Britannica." I played along. It is possible that I even named more than one, as some of the smarter kids in my class were doing. It pleased the teacher and was surprisingly easy.

Then one day, all the kids came to school carrying construction paper maps. Behind each map was a report. They were beautiful. More to the point, everybody had one except me.

Perhaps most people would look askance at my qualifications as a teacher. They might be surprised to find out that my favorite subject is history. This is simply because I am discovering the material along with my children.

My main sources are pre-Seventies Catholic textbooks. Such texts, authored by nuns, usually take up a third of the population on homeschool bookshelves, just being edged out by classic works of literature.

Among other things, you can read about the fascinating history of Brazil: the tug of war between Portugal and Spain; how the Pope called for a map of the world and a pen and proceeded to do like the auto club giving directions — drawing a line down the middle, apportioning what looked like half of the New World to one and half to the other. Enter the Jesuits doing spiritual battle against paganism and greed for the souls of these future coffee exporters, and it's exciting enough to be in the movies. For the ethnic background, there's our Brazilian friend Joao — whose features are a mixture of Native American, African, and Portuguese. In his expression you see Christianity.

It's a pity that the consensus among most American adults and children is that history contains nothing but a boring montage of names, dates, facts, figures, and battles that have nothing to do with us today. I prefer to think of history as beginning with Adam and ending with the last *Amen* in Revelation. There is a lot that goes on in between, and all of it is meaningful in light of the coming of the God-man. History is part of religion.

As with Brazil, it was years before I got interested in the obscure African tribes we had been treated to in ninth grade. Back then, our class found them entertaining for the sole reason that they had nothing on but face paint. Later, through the lens of the missionary saints, they became men — rational redeemed men whom God was very much interested in. Men who will stand beside me at the general judgment. In that light, even their average income and the products they export become interesting.

As far as teaching style goes, I also diverge from my honorable forebores. I have an embarrassing flair for the dramatic — nourished, no doubt, by years of daydreaming in Social Studies class.

I portray the peoples of the past as ordinary folks given extraordinary roles to play. They did the same sorts of things we do, only with vastly more important consequences. In the Old Testament, there is a tale of King Assuerus having a bout with insomnia. He called one of his servants and asked him to bring the chronicles. He was reading in bed to get to sleep! And the only reading material to be had in those days were the chronicles. They were pretty juicy, too, because in them the king discovered that the man who was scheduled for execution the next day had once saved his life!

Please Don't Drink the Holy Water!

But in my mind, nothing is wackier than the truce between El Adil, son of Saladin, and King Richard the Lionhearted. According to the history books, the truce was to last three years, three months, three weeks, three days, three hours, three minutes, and three seconds. While no one seems to know why, I couldn't help filling in the possibilities. . . .

Third Crusade

El Adil: Okay, let me get this straight. You want me to quit grinding your army into powder to give you time to recover so that you can come back and wipe us all out?

Richard: Exactly.

El Adil: Well . . . that seems reasonable enough. How long will you need?

Richard: Hmmm . . . let's see. . . . Bury the dead, then pack and get the wounded shaped up and shipped out, several months for the trip home, time to kick my brother John off my throne and straighten things up there. Might even take a month off to spend time with the family. Meanwhile, the Pope will want to send more guys. . . . Then there are the guns, ships, and return trip — I got it. How's three years?

El Adil: Take all the time you need! Why not three years and three months?

Richard: Why not three years, three months, and three weeks?

El Adil: Tell you what: I'll throw in three days.

Richard: How about three hours?

El Adil: I can top that: how about three hours and three minutes?

Richard: Make that three seconds, and you've got a deal.

El Adil: It's a deal. Let's have another drink on it.

Richard: Here's to meeting again under better conditions!

Both: *Clink!*

C U R R E N T S

Newsletter of F.I.S.H. —
Forming and Inspiring through Schooling at Home

Annual F.I.S.H. Musical

Once again it is time for F.I.S.H. to put on its annual musical! This year we are staging *A Man for All Seasons.* We already have several girls who are interested in playing Lady Margaret. Because of the few other female roles available, girls with alto voices may be asked to fill male parts. The role of the executioner is still wide open. Parents with large homes or skills in acting, directing, lighting, choreography, costume design, and carpentry are asked to step forward. We will also need mothers to bake cookies for this event.

Rugby Player Wanted

The O'Brien boys are looking to form a rugby team, but as their youngest brother is still in diapers, they are short one player. If your son weighs over 150 pounds, this is an excellent way to get phys-ed into his curriculum. Please bring liability waiver.

Trigger Finger School Tour

It is not too late to sign up for our tour of Trigger Fingers Middle School. Even though school is dismissed for vacation,

several students of Trigger have been
detained and have graciously offered to
donate a portion of the bathroom wall
for graffiti instruction. Because of the
large group we are expecting, however,
only late arrivals will be permitted to
write on the wall. Officials from the
city will also be on hand to demonstrate
a search and seizure in the locker area.
Students are requested to hand over their
lunch money on arrival.

Leaflet Distributors Needed

Mrs. Eketiana Stavroupolos is running again
for senator on the Family Values Party
ticket. She is looking for help distribut-
ing leaflets door-to-door to 500,000 people
before noon next Tuesday. Even with no
budget, she managed to garner one percent
of the vote last time, so this year her
chances are even greater. It's a wonderful
opportunity to get the message out, shed a
few extra pounds, and learn firsthand about
the effectiveness of our two-party system.

***

Real Answers
from Real Moms

This month's answer comes from Marge
Hubbard. To the question "What do you do
if your teenage daughter has a trashy teen

idol poster on her wall?" Marge replies, "Wait until her friends are over and bring in little brother and his friends to make fun of it. If you do not have your own little brother, a big brother, if he is sarcastic enough, might do. If not, borrow a little brother from one of your friends. You are welcome to any or all six of mine anytime." Thanks, Marge!

Next month's question is "Why are St. Lucy's eyes on a plate and in her head, too?" Please e-mail answers, conjectures, and wisecracks to realmama@home.net.

***

Sales Corner

Tropical-rainforest kit, never used. Original cost: $300. Need pick-up truck. If you can haul it, you can have it — free! Call Lucinda Spender. Hurry! She hopes it won't last.

—

Trigger Fingers Middle School is unloading another **year's supply of used desks**. With a little elbow grease and a big sander, the gum and profanities come right off. A bargain at $10 apiece.

—

Math Cuisenaire Rods. These provide tactile help in teaching math and are expensive in catalogs. Not recommended for households

with children under three. The Choker Family says make us an offer.

—

First-grade curriculum from Our Lady of
Perpetual Work Homeschool. Box includes
everything your six-year-old needs to make
it into Harvard next year. Unopened. Slight
damage around edges due to impact when
crane dropped it onto porch. Please send
donation in lieu of flowers to the Jane
Crush Memorial Fund.

—

Need **Chicken Pox**? Great news: The Lloyds
are scheduled to **break out** within the next
several days. Act now! Offer good while
disease lasts.

***

Mother's Proverb

A woman's age is as unimportant
as the size of her shoes
which grows with each
  successive child.
If her driving vision is unimpaired
and she possesses crock pot and bread
  machine,
To be several children young
is sometimes
far more cheerful and hopeful
than to be twenty-three years old.
           — *Olivia Wellness Home*

∞

Aquinas on Homeschooling

If homeschooling had been a point of controversy in Aquinas's day, it certainly would have made it into the *Summa* — which, translated from Latin, means literally, the book which contains every question that can be thought up.

Question:
WHETHER HOMESCHOOLING IS
THE PROPER FORM OF EDUCATION

We thus proceed to the first article:

Objection 1: It would seem that homeschooling is *not* the proper form of education because children by nature must leave home at a young age to be educated by strangers.

Objection 2: Further, every child has a right to a lunchbox, preferably with cartoon characters on it and a thermos inside.

Objection 3: Further, it is crucial to the formation of a child's character for the rest of his life that he meet "kids his own age" in a classroom setting.

Objection 4: Further, all teachers are qualified and nice and motivating, and if they are not, that works out okay, too, because, hey, that's the Real World. Get used to it, kid.

Objection 5: Further, when kids reach school age, a mother is supposed to "have her own life." (For a definition of "own life," see Friedan, ch. 11, vs. 666.)

Objection 6: Further, after seeing her child off to school, the mother is supposed to drive a sleek little set of wheels to a six-figure career in a climate-controlled office. Or she may go to work in a mail-sorting warehouse. This is more fulfilling than staying home and doing nothing all day.

Objection 7: Further, when children are absent, a mother regains her youth and vitality and sustains it for an indefinite period or until they come home, whichever comes first.

Objection 8: Further, family harmony flourishes when children are away because each individual member is fulfilled, and besides, too much togetherness in one family leads to mutilation.

Objection 9: Further, a mother who attempts homeschooling thinks she is too good for everybody else, and that is just plain un-American.

On the contrary: It is written, Shut up, and mind your own business.

I answer that: When faced with the above objections, a mother may try one of three options. (See *Pocket Summa* Workbook Edition, 900th printing.)

A. She can go around telling people she's not a snob. *Warning:* Combining this with an attitude of confidence is hazardous to your health.

B. She can pretend she doesn't think what she's doing is really the best thing. I mean, well, like, not for *everybody*.

C. She can start dressing like a leftover hippie. Homeschoolers who look like hippies are acceptable because they are not thought to be homeschooling for religious reasons.

If option C is chosen, she may exchange it for what's behind Door Number One.[1]

---

[1] An overcrowded used minivan.

∞

The Sheep and the Goats

Do you ever wonder why our Lord compares His faithful to sheep? I discovered the answer one day while listening to Handel's *Messiah* which, quoting Isaiah states, "All we like sheep, all we like sheep, all we like sheep, we have turn-ed, we have turn-ed, we have turn-ed, we have turn-ed, everyone to his own way, everyone to his own, to his own way." Isaiah's message, despite a stuttering problem, is plain. It has to do with the scattered-flock mentality. But our similarity to the beast does not end there.

In college, my friends and I watched a flock of sheep grazing on a hillside in Liechtenstein. We were philosophers in those days, able to glean insight into human nature from any source whatsoever.

The first thing we noticed was how different sheep are from one another. For one thing, they don't all go, "Baa, baa" at middle C as you might expect. A few of them do the traditional bleat, but the majority are somewhere in the range of two octaves above or below. Size seems to be the determining factor there. The very little lambs had a delightfully cute, high-pitched "mi-mi" stutter. The ewes reprimanded them in guttural tones that betrayed a pack-a-day smoking habit, while the large males sounded like Mafia bosses who hadn't been paid.

Please Don't Drink the Holy Water!

The flock was milling about contentedly within their parameters even with no shepherd in sight. They showed no signs of going every one to his own way, every one to his — well, you get it — as long as the grazing was good.

The only thing they wanted out of us higher beings was that we keep off the grass. And every last one of them was wearing dung on wool that season.

The whole thing was rather embarrassing.

Sheep, I am told, are extremely dependent creatures. They follow one another around with their heads down, making sure to keep the foregoing sheep's behind in full view. Each one is banking on the foregoing sheep having more knowledge of the shepherd's whereabouts than he has.

Goats, on the other hand, from close scientific observations of mine (while extracting my skirt from a goat's mouth at a petting zoo), appear much more to the advantage. Unlike sheep, they are liberated beings. Goats believe in themselves. Why not? You can't tie them up. They have razor-rapid teeth, and their stomachs can digest anything. They're cute and clean besides. I must confess a certain admiration of their rugged individualism. They remind me of myself. Their little hooves are built for climbing slick narrow cliffs where they perch with a look of blind pride just before a loose rock gives and hurls them into an open gorge.

I guess our Lord was saying that whether following the crowd or branching out on our own, we really don't know what we are doing. We'd best trust Him.

Take Catholics today.

In the pre-Vatican II olden days, you could tell a Catholic by the uniform. Children wore plaid, nuns sported a habit and another nun; priests, a backward collar, black pants suit, big ears, and a smooth singing voice. Catholic storybook mothers wore dresses, gloves, and black pumps to hang laundry. They wore the same thing in the kitchen, except for exchanging gloves for apron. Fathers wore authority, standing head and shoulders above everyone except the parish priest. Dad's accessories included a large gunmetal lunch box and choice of briefcase or tractor.

Hey, Hollywood still uses some of it, but not much of it reflects the Real World.

Even Catholics who reside in Shelterhaven don't always fit the description. We wear the same uniform as the rest of the world; for the layperson, a T-shirt and jeans. Priests usually preserve distinction with a polo-shirt-and-khakis ensemble. In the Seventies, you could spot a nun a mile off by her polyester blazer and lapel pin. Today they have virtually disappeared from the landscape. Maybe there isn't really a vocation shortage. Perhaps they've just acquired taste.

A friend and I were at a large homeschool meeting last year. It was one of those events where you expect to find a bunch of people who look and talk alike.

The group looked more diverse than a can of mixed nuts.

A few arrived in regulation jean jumper. Some were dressed for church. Others wore jeans.

If you got past wardrobe and into conversation, you would discover that religiously, the gamut didn't run; it galloped. The majority were conservative Novus Ordo. (Before we go on, let me interject that we are now entering the tunnel of subdistinction. "Conservative Novus Ordo" can mean the Mass of Paul VI in Latin, or it can mean Anything Goes if the pastor is pro-life.) Besides this group, there were a few Byzantine refugees representing the Melkite, Ruthenian, and Ukrainian Rites. There was a growing Tridentine corner, mostly indults, a smattering of Pius Xs, two or three Pius Vs, and one very vocal Pius II ½ — although she was thinking of dropping the half. Most shocking of all was a large group of Saturday-night moderates, but it turned out they were all in one family.

Speaking of families, no two raised their kids alike.

Some were diehard no TV, no computer. A few had monitors just for movies. I overheard one woman admit she had a satellite dish to somebody who had just cut the cable. The woman hastened to add that it was for educational purposes only.

There were Tridentines who looked Amish and kid lectors in belly shirts and hip-huggers, and vice versa.

A heated debate flared up over at the pro-life table: whether to vote for the real pro-lifer who didn't have a chance and take votes away from the lesser of two evils who did have a chance, *or* vote for the lesser evil and make it impossible for the real pro-lifer to have a chance. The discussion ended when one side accused the other of infanticide.

One fold and one shepherd?

This is not to say there are no right answers. There categorically are. And hey, if you want to know what they are, you only have to ask me!

Part 2

∞

Driving Under the Influence of Guilt

∞

The Top Ten Things
That Resist Societal Change

Homeschoolers and/or traditionally minded Catholics are often accused of being out of touch with the Real World. This is somewhat true. Our family, for one, consistently ignores fads. Maybe this comes from being raised Catholic in the Seventies when experimentation was the only consistent feature of Mass with Fr. La Mode. Greg and I go for the tried and true, the things that can be counted on to last.

Not just in the most important things like liturgy and politics, but in the small stuff. We couldn't tell you where we were and what we were doing when hoards of people stood in line for hours to get Tickle Me Elmo. Probably watching a *Honeymooners* rerun. When people went wild about Harry Potter and others were issuing a swift denunciation, we couldn't even generate mild curiosity. We were right in the middle of the Narnia series at the time. People were gyrating to the Macarena just when Greg and I began taking ballroom-dancing lessons.

It's not that we can't keep up with the Real World and its ever-changing fads. It's just that we find the stuff that lasts a lot more interesting.

Please Don't Drink the Holy Water!

For instance:

1. *Kids discover a keen scientific interest in* National Geographic. Somehow we got hold of three old issues of *National Geographic.* We're not sure how they got on our shelves. Possibly they were planted by cross-pollination, because they sprang up like weeds in the midst of a field of wholesome Catholic magazines that have no naked pictures in them. One day we found the kids giggling helplessly all over the floor and knew that we had witnessed a milestone of growing up. The funniest part was when they let us in on their discovery. We hated to tell them that we already knew all about it. The only behavioral difference between us and them was that neither Greg nor I mentioned it to our parents. Kids who show their folks naked pictures. Just one more benefit of homeschooling.

2. *When your kids mature, you will suddenly lapse into incompetence.* Even if you have never missed a day of feeding, clothing, and providing shelter for your family, your kids will reach an age where they are really not sure that you know what you're doing. In firstborn children, this has been known to start as young as nine years old. They will ask you if you know where you're going, if you're sure about the time, whether you've called ahead, flushed the toilet, washed your hands, turned off the light, locked up, and if you are sure which key turns on the ignition.

3. *Around adults, teenagers slow their pulse to coma level.* In an effort to combat being thought of as weird, the average teenager will take care to show no emotion whatsoever on his face when around anyone outside of his peer group — especially responsible adults. This personality-deprived condition would appear to be serious if it weren't known to be temporary. In extreme cases of coolness, however, slack faces have been known to get stuck.

The Top Ten Things That Resist Societal Change

4. Three-year-olds find the potty irresistible whenever it is most inconvenient.

• *When dressed in several layers of clothing.* This includes snow overalls, jacket, mittens, hat, and dripping wet boots.

• *During the Rosary.* A potty break is good for at least a decade. An extremely helpful older child will often volunteer to help. By the way, this is the same kid who thinks saying, "Death, amen," is the minimum requirement to have completed a Hail Mary.

• *When food arrives at a restaurant.* After waiting a half-hour through arrival, ordering, and service, child wishes to make sure mother's meal is just the way she eats it at home — lukewarm.

• *At a park.* Provided the lavatories are all locked and there is a McDonald's tastefully hidden in the recesses of a mall at least three miles away.

• *At Mass.* Not during the Sign of Peace, not right as people file up and down for Communion, not even when the collection is being taken. This would make it too easy to get up and leave without disturbing anyone. The time of choice is when everyone is kneeling silently or the priest is preaching.

• *When Mom is in the bathroom.* Groans and the sound of jumping will be heard along with the question, "What are you doing in there?"

• *At movies, piano recitals, outdoor concerts, indoor concerts, plays, ballgames, and anywhere you cannot use a pause button to stop the show temporarily.*

5. *Lent is the homeschooler's darkest hour before the dawn.* It will always coincide with months that are dark, cold, and damp. For the homeschooler, it arrives when there are still ninety-seven days left of a 180-day school year.

6. *Things you don't want your kids to have will be purchased for them by others.*

• *For boys:* guns, machetes, flamethrowers, grenades, and other non-environmentally friendly killing devices.

• *For girls:* Bikini Bimbo Barbie.

• And then there are huge plastic toys that take over your starter home or apartment. These come in assorted flavors. Solid plastic, uncollapsible, containing several screws and directions. Accessorized by a carry bag for convenient storage. You might as well go ahead and set fire to this carry bag on the first day because, once unpacked, the toy will not fit back into it.

7. *More money will be urgently needed to invent new programs for distressed public schools* — implementing daring measures such as the outlawing of pajamas in class, and reducing competition by eliminating grades and other potentially divisive distinctions. Then there is breakfast, lunch, and dinner to provide, afterschool and summer programs to make full use of the buildings, not to mention ever-increasing salaries for teachers who oppose tax credits for the private sector because "it's public money."

8. *People with large families are doomed to watch reruns.* The dialogue in these reruns goes, "Better you than me"; "So, are you done?"; and "You have your hands full." No matter how many times your ears have heard these comments, you have to humor

these people because they really do innocently think they are being original. You know this because their eyes are bugging out and they are gasping as if in shock.

9. *Kids do their part to contribute to a chaotic situation.* If you're rushing out the door to get somewhere on time while the phone is ringing, the pot boiling over, and the dog barking, kids will add to the chaos. Ours provide appropriate background music. When little, they banged on the piano. Now that they've had years of lessons, they pound out the boogiest tune in their repertoire. In cases where a piano is not to be had, never fear; they can always sing and march around and twirl long-handled objects.

10. *Motherhood comes with automatic rocking hips.* These hips rock everything between ten and thirty pounds, even if it does not remotely resemble a baby: brown paper grocery sacks (you just can't get intimate with the plastic ones, besides they have handles), a bowling ball, a knapsack stuffed with library books. Anything they have to hold while standing around for more than thirty seconds.

∞

How to Get Rid of Scam Artists, Mormons, and Other People You've Unwittingly Moved in Next Door To

I came from Suburbia. Yes, it was the quintessential boringly safe, predictable sort of place where you could leave your doors and windows wide open while you were out and fear nothing worse than a flash midsummer thunderstorm that filled your house with two feet of water and split your gigantic maple tree in half.

Now that I am married, kidfull, and living in a city row home that is attached to several other city row homes, there is far more at risk than carpeting, drapes, woodwork, furniture, marriage license, the deed to your house, pictures of dead relatives dating back to the dawn of photography, and whatever else you left by an open window. Your money, for one.

The first five years we were in our house, word traveled among local scam artists that new suckers had been born that very minute. First there was the young guy who came to the door on a dark evening just when I was expecting my husband to come home. I threw the door open wide to see not Greg's familiar face, but that of a shadowy stranger holding a roll of paper towels. He and his buddy, out in the van, just wanted to show me some handy household products. Could they come in? Maybe it was my guardian angel, or maybe it was the fact that I've never heard of a door-to-door paper-towel salesman, but I got the willies. I quickly stammered, "No, thanks," slammed the door in their face, locked it, and started thinking seriously about getting a dog — or at least a barking doorbell.

Then there was a woman collecting for hurricane victims I had never heard of, who was so nervous I can only conclude I was her very first shakedown.

My personal favorite was a woman wearing wig, head scarf, and dark glasses who wanted to know if I was "interested in world peace" enough to add to her wad, as all of my neighbors whose names I didn't recognize had. Through various well-crafted arguments beginning and ending with "Get outta here before I call the cops," I managed to persuade her to get outta there.

Then one day a guy who "just ran out of gas down the street, can I have fifteen bucks and I'll bring you back thirty" — yeah, right — came to the door. It must have been a Saturday, because he got my husband instead of me. He also got five bucks and our gas can. I was glad Greg had handed over only five instead of fifteen, but having to go buy a new gas can really bugged me. Greg apologetically offered to walk to the nearest Home Depot (the car was out of gas) to buy a new one. I told him, "Don't bother. Just catch up with the guy and get directions to his house, because you know he has about two hundred empty gas cans in his backyard." Later we heard that the guy made the local paper for slugging a resistant tightwad in another neighborhood he was canvassing. So Greg and I concluded that it is sometimes better to be a sucker than to be sucker-punched.

Our worst experience was when a professional extortionist moved into our row. He scammed everybody in the row except my immediate neighbors who were lucky enough to be foreigners trying to eke out a meager living in a strange land where they didn't know the language. Our turn came on an icy winter day, as my husband was idling our van down our back alley. Although the neighbor testified later that he had seen my husband in the road, he whizzed his car right into his path nonetheless, leaving no choice for my husband but to hit him.

The guy sustained only a broken turn-signal light — for which he then demanded five hundred dollars because he figured he'd get his door fixed while he was at it. Now, to the privilege of being educated to have full command of the English tongue (not to mention German and Russian), Greg adds the gift of blarney, which came over from Ireland with Granny McTaggert's baggage. Soon Greg was batting the guy around verbally like a cat playing with a mouse. Our neighbor withdrew in frustration, and later, when he called from an undisclosed location to bark incriminating threats into the phone, he lost all hope of getting money and instead got a visit from the police.

Our house also used to be a target of door-to-door heretics. How refreshing — for once, people who were not trying to steal anything from me but my soul! There were many things I admired about them — their guts, their lovely manners, their wardrobe. And I told them so. "That's a sharp suit, lady. Even with the door propped open just the width of your shoe I can tell it coordinates beautifully with that briefcase. . . . What's that? No, I don't want a copy of *Look Out Below* magazine."

With such a beautiful opener, I then proceed to defend my Faith as best I can through the three inches of space, sticking to the two main rules of Catholic apologetics.

Rule number one is not to let the elegant visitor lead you down her twisted road, but to take up the offense. Greg tried this once by telling a Jehovah's Witness, who was a former Catholic, that our Lord scandalized him. "No way!" The guy insisted. "Nothing our Lord said would ever scandalize me!" Greg grabbed the guy's mutilated Bible and read him John 6 — where Christ says His flesh is food indeed. The guy leapt from the porch, ran in midair for five seconds, then dissolved into a streak, leaving nothing but a blue vapor in his place.

Rule number two is to educate yourself about the peculiar beliefs of the sect represented by said elegant visitor squished inside your storm door. This will prepare you to converse with Mormons who promise you your own planet in the afterlife and Scientologists living in fear of the galactic overlord Xenu. But well-prepared as I am, I still get stumped sometimes, as I was in this conversation with a Jehovah's Witness:

> J.W.: Do you believe Jesus is the A-Man?
> Educated Catholic: Huh?
> J.W.: It says in the Bible that He is.
> Educated Catholic: Whaa?
> J.W.: Right at the end.

Finally it dawned on me that she was referring to the word *Amen* and the end of Revelation. I tried telling her that it meant "So be it," or according to the latest ICEL translation, "Whatever." But she was glancing anxiously at her watch, which matched perfectly with her Nubuck shoes and handbag in taupe and dewy rose.

> J.W.: Well, thank you for giving me some of your time. I will now exit swiftly without losing the least bit of my composure. I have something to ask one of the elders. I will never return. However, you can look forward to another elegant visitor who will pose an equally challenging question to you.

Mormons have a much better sales pitch, and I mean, even without the special offer (available only while supplies last) of getting to be king of your own planet. I've had the pleasure of only one visit, and I must say I really blew it. My girls were quite small and helpless (if you don't count demolition skills), my husband not home quite often enough to do yard work. And lo! Here were not one, but two extremely healthy-looking, polite young men wearing bicycles and backpacks on my doorstep. They claimed to be sent from God, and they asked if they could *do* anything for me!!

I did have quite a bit of weeding and bagging for them to do, but instead of recognizing them as an answer to my prayers, all I said was, "I don't think so. I'm Roman Catholic," with a touch of fatalistic unworthiness in my voice. They looked at me sympathetically and said, "Oh really? Well that's cool. Bye." On the way down the steps I thought I saw them shaking the dust from their bike tires.

As I said, our house used to be a target. It has been many moons since any Mormons or Jehovah's Witnesses have tried to sell me my own planet or guarantee me a spot on the New Earth, all expenses paid by the A-Man.

Perhaps the credit goes to my husband, who gallantly killed off many a yard-working Saturday to explain the truths of our Faith from the Bible. Even though his challengers left unconvinced after three hours, his subsequent martyrdom at my hands must have merited some grace with God.

Or perhaps it was the times they had rung the doorbell, seen the curtains move, and heard scurrying from within our house as the children and I dove under the bed that finally convinced them of our invincible doom.

∞

For All the Saints

As I see it, opinion on how to celebrate Halloween is divided into roughly four camps. In one you have Evangelicals and some Catholics who respond to the roaming ghouls and devils by shutting off the porch light and distracting their kids until the coast is clear. Opposite this is the general population of folks who see nothing in it but dressing up, collecting candy, and saying hi to the neighbors; this camp includes plenty of Christians but mostly seculars who have no idea that hallows are saints and that an "een" is an eve. Then you've got retailers whose sole mission around any holiday is to persuade everybody that they need to "stock up while supplies last."

Then there's the compromise class — into which stumbles my family.

We're tradition-minded Catholics who, while realizing that Halloween has gone the way of most holidays — namely, from pagan to Catholic and back again — still want our kids to have a little fun.

On Halloween, we've always done the saint thing. This was my idea to get Greg to let the kids go trick-or-treating. Since it meant evangelizing the whole neighborhood, he went for it.

The yearly challenge has always been to come up with original ideas without compromising our family tradition. I'm sure a lot of fellow die-hards go through this.

The first two options that scream, "Pick me!" when you have girls are the Blessed Mother or a nun. But I've always hesitated. Nuns are already fodder for caricature; it wouldn't do if people thought we were making fun of them. Besides, with nun costumes in stores, they're not all that original. When we have done them, it was as specifics — St. Thérèse of Lisieux (complete with roses and cross) and Elizabeth Seton (the habit of mourning lends interest). When it comes to the Blessed Mother, specialization is also the key to originality. Guadalupe and LaSalette are rich in imagery. So are all of the metaphoric titles in the Litany of Loretto — Gate of Heaven, Seat of Wisdom, Ark of the Covenant — but we lack basic carpentry skills.

Without specialization, there are only so many nuns, so many blue and white Mary bathrobes, and so many nondescriptly robed saints that can be done before boredom sets in. To add to the difficulty, our possibilities are cut in half. I've tried, but none of the girls wants to play John the Baptist, with or without the platter.

Themes are a help. One year we did the Fatima kids; two girls went as Lucia and Jacinta, and one consented to go as Francisco, carrying a flute. The baby was a lamb.

The next year we recycled the lamb and one of the shepherdess outfits and sent somebody as St. Germaine.

The next year with the "baby" bursting out of the lamb suit and the shepherd theme duly spent, we again faced a challenge.

The Old Testament opened up a whole world of possibilities. I've always had a hankering to dress as Moses myself: long beard, white hair, bushy eyebrows, and the telltale stone tablets, just in case the neighbors don't get it. Recycle the wig and eyebrows and

you can do Noah, with a dove on his shoulder and a cardboard
boat built around him. A little clumsy for handing out candy . . .
but cool, and very original.

We did send one of our girls as Isaac's wife Rebecca, in the recycled shepherdess dress replete with gold bracelets and carrying a
golden jug.

But it was getting old. There was no denying it.

Next we rode the queen circuit. Plenty of possibilities there —
the biblical Esther, Elizabeth of Hungary, Zita of Austria, Isabella
of Spain — not all canonized saints, but close enough. The pitfall
is that without precise period costumes and hair, they all manage
to look alike, even if they're hundreds of years apart.

Of course, there is always good old reliable Kateri Tekakwitha.
A lot of girls in our homeschool group did her the year Pocahontas
costumes were in the stores.

One year my girls were in Little Flowers — a sort of Girl Scouts
for Catholics — so we decided to branch off and do the virtues.
This amounted to a fairy-princess look based on the flower that
matched the virtue (e.g., sunflower = faith). The dresses were gorgeous, but for some reason our adolescent found the whole thing
embarrassing.

The next year, we went further out on a limb and sent our kids
as occupations. The idea was that for every occupation there is a
patron saint. One was a doctor in honor of St. Luke, an artist for
Bl. Fra Angelico, and so on.

I thought it was good. It was the first time they looked like the
rest of the kids in the neighborhood. The kids liked the theme at
the time, but it didn't go down in history as one of their favorites.

I still think it holds promise. If you wanted to go as a street ur-
chin, you could be Matt Talbot; a hiker, Giorgio Frassati; a skater,
Tara Lipinski (okay, she's not a saint, but she's a good Catholic by

all accounts), a pirate . . . well, there must be some saint somewhere who is the patron of pirates — repentant, of course.

Then the Holy Ghost threw me a lifeline. Everybody got
hooked on *Lord of the Rings*. The fact that Tolkien was a Catholic
and that the books were loosely allegorical was a godsend. I must
admit our eldest, with her long blond hair slicked back, looked every bit like Legolas. For the first time in quite a while, everyone
agreed that this was cool.

After that, I promised them we'd do Lewis's allegorical characters. There are seven books in the Narnia series! As luck would
have it, I spied a lion costume on sale in a local department
store. Aslan — a figure of Jesus, "not a tame lion" — was por-
trayed by our two-year-old. It was the first Halloween costume I
have ever purchased and, I must say, a blessed relief. Our second
eldest was a Narnian tree spirit; the third Aravis the Tarkheena,
dressed as a boy; the fourth, her Narnian horse, Hwin. And to
think I did it all with a glue gun. I offered our eldest the White
Witch as a part of the theme, but she chose instead to be a
Narnian queen. Somehow it got ingrained in our children to go as
holy things. Apparently the way we've brought them up has
formed their imaginations the way we intended. An amazing
phenomenon.

As for the future, I'm already fermenting some ideas. Thinking
back to my childhood when I painted a box to look like a pack of
Wrigley's gum and climbed into it gave me the idea of going as sacred objects. No patens or chalices, mind you; that would not be
kosher. Things like a candle, or even an incense burner — add a
little dry ice and think of the possibilities!

A friend suggested going as a soul in Purgatory. A largish costume encased, as it were, in flames, with a grimacing face barely
breaking out. Sounds rather like a series of unfinished Pietàs by

Michelangelo that I once saw in Florence. Cool, original, and kinda scary.

If you really want to be ghoulish, how about relics? I once was blessed by St. Fidelis's skull. If you wanted to go way out, you could wear a skull with a reliquary around it. If you find suffocation a problem, you might look into St. Ignatius's arm. It's in a golden, arm-shaped reliquary in the Church of the Gesu in Rome.

This brings me back to the All Souls motif introduced by my friend. It does open up a whole new type of costume idea. For All Souls, you can actually use the traditional skeleton and ghost thing. Heck, you can be almost anybody who has made it at least as far as Purgatory — even a mobster with a deathbed repentance.

So how has all of this served the cause of evangelization? Well, one lady did recognize our midget version of St. Thérèse and was properly edified. Largely, however, nobody notices. My husband was terribly disappointed. One year, to combat this ignorance, he had the girls sing "For All the Saints" at every house. They came back an hour later with seven pieces of candy. Our adolescent had even less. Even candy couldn't induce her to take part. That was almost our last Halloween, but for the pledge I exacted from Greg with torture.

But I do sympathize with his point. What is all this dress-up for but to be noticed? Of all the things people find intolerable about Halloween, my pet peeve is the way kids come to the door and gape at me with one hand out. I always grin and cup my ear and wait for "Trick-or-treat." After that I insist on "Thank you." Hey, if you don't educate them, kids will think this is just another commercial holiday where they get a handout for no apparent reason.

We've managed, these umpteen Halloweens, to stick to the Catholicity of the day in spite of hints by our more mainstream Catholic friends that such a thing would be no fun and horribly

"And who are you supposed to be, dear?"

uncreative. After Narnia last year, the kids surprised us by asking for a return of the saints for next year. They missed them. They had been their companions every Halloween. They spoke of the cos-tumes they had loved — Kateri, Guadalupe, Seton. I was floored. To them the saints have always been *fun*.

∞

Forbidden Fruits

I've always wondered why our Lord insisted that heaven is a banquet. Maybe it was because He was talking to a bunch of men. Consider, for a moment, what men do on holidays — kick back, eat, do a few deep knee bends, eat some more, see which team is winning, eat some more, drink, and eat. They don't plan it, shop it, cook it, or clean it up. Very seldom do they feed it to the baby or pick it out of his hair. No wonder the banquet imagery got so many male converts.

The real reason our Lord did not pick women apostles was because He knew that somewhere in the congregation a hand would have shot up — "Rabbi, I know that I am privileged to be a part of this. That hundreds of years from now, people will wish they had been in my place, sitting here at Your feet, listening to You discuss the inexplicable joys that await those who love You. I just need a clarification here. Who is throwing this party? Oh — the angels? I see. Well, that's fine. Just wanted to make sure You had planners, shoppers, cooks, and dishwashers lined up, especially because this is going to be an eternal affair. And one more thing: I won't have to feel guilty if I don't pitch in, will I? Great. Which way to the River Jordan?"

Please Don't Drink the Holy Water!

A lot of women I know think of eating as a necessary evil. Keep in mind that these women are skirt-wearing, Rosary-saying types, who thought Hillary Clinton's remark about the little woman who baked cookies was demeaning. They, and this includes me, would, under normal conditions, love to bake cookies. It's fun. It makes our families feel warm and fuzzy, and nothing beats the taste of raw dough. But if you introduce the demands of a large family, the hassles of eating far outweigh the benefits.

On the pro side, it keeps you alive.

On the con side, you have creative planning, shopping, preparation, and cleanup — all for an hour of pleasure. When you factor in the children, out goes the hour of pleasure. When I'm not force-feeding a picky toddler, I'm nagging my older kids to stop talking with their mouths open or stop eating with their mouths full. It doesn't have to make sense, because my mouth's usually full when I say it.

"Girls, don't eat with your mouth full!"

Now, I know as an American I am privileged to live in a country that takes great national pride in its variety of cuisines. Still, sometimes I look with envy on simple cultures with simple diets. In primitive cultures, kids didn't ask what was for dinner and then immediately complain about it. Why? Because the answer never varied. Nobody thought of saying, "Aw, roasted missionary again?!" It was understood that you ate whatever abundance God sent you.

Now, I do know a few women who like to cook. For them it's a hobby, not a life sentence.

When I was single, I was in that category. I enjoyed leafing through domestic magazines looking for exotic recipes like kiwi-almond casserole with a side of mint. Then, I would go to the store and select just the right ingredients. The most alluring recipes always wore a skimpy little getup like, "Preparation time: 20 minutes." This is probably true if you don't have to stop to look up the meaning of *blanching, parboiling, poaching, frying,* and *baking,* and how to turn the oven on. With the effort I put out, one might expect to create something good enough to serve the entire staff of the White House. Yet after five hours, it yielded only four servings and looked nothing like the picture. But it did taste just as revolting as the name suggested.

These sorts of projects continued into marriage because I so wanted to impress my husband. Our first stove was a hot plate with two burners, which necessitated a diet of boiled starch, fried meat, and canned vegetables. The only fancy thing I ever tried was broccoli in spaghetti. Even though I now cook worth my salt, my husband still teases me about it to this day.

He also likes to razz me about the amounts of food I'd make back then. To feed both of us, it seemed logical to cook double what I would normally eat. I weighed 102 pounds. Pretty soon my husband did, too. Luckily, pregnancy solved the problem, and my appetite grew to match his.

Even after we moved to a place with an oven, my troubles were not over. Food did not regenerate itself, and we didn't have a car. But I have always been a resourceful person. Once I ran so low that I threw a blanket on the living room floor and we had a picnic with raisins, peanuts, apples, and beer. My husband went along with it cheerfully enough, but I've never had the guts to try it again — especially when we're out of beer.

If only I had realized that God never cut me out for high-tech domesticity, I would have saved myself a lot of guilt. It was a relief when my mother told me she cooked nothing but hot dogs for the first year of her married life.

By the time I came along, she had several meat and potato recipes capable of feeding a whole neighborhood. She also had five sons.

God has taken pity on me by giving me five daughters. Daughters don't have the same needs as sons. They can live for days on hors d'oeuvres. You can present just about anything on a cute tray with teacups beside it, and they will squeal with delight. With daughters, it is also possible to ration milk. My brothers, on the other hand, thought they were helping their mother when they drank the last quart of milk right from the carton so as to avoid getting a glass dirty.

God gave me daughters, but he made my husband a boy.

For a while, I was counting my blessings because my husband is a pasta lover. Nothing is easier, faster, or cheaper. When he gets bored with that, there's always rice or potatoes — preferably smothered in cream sauce or cheese. This is known as the Fatkins Diet.

Fatkins is a major part of a complete homeschool diet.

Then one day, one of my husband's friends dropped the *F*. And with it went any chance of convincing his children that he was Santa Claus that year. Proteins were where it was *at*. Then another friend tried it, then another. . . . As soon as they traded carbs for abs, these guys got evangelistic. They were off pasta, bread, spuds, rice, and beer and claimed to feel great.

At the same time, some of my women friends started preaching a diet of their own. It was a no-dye, no-preservative, low-sugar diet guaranteed to end mood swings, counteract the alphabet syndrome in children, and prevent diseases induced by the quick fixes that make up the other half of the complete homeschool diet.

Suddenly I realized that I had been killing my family. I, who should have known better.

You see, when I was eleven, my father suffered a heart attack. A year later, my mother contracted cancer. Their response to these life-threatening diseases was a radical change of diet. They read every package carefully for mention of monosodium glutamate, nitrates, red dye number five, and hormones. This cut out all snacks that came wrapped in plastic. Ice cream, my mom's favorite food, was unfortunately made with stuff that they (Real World types) put in paint thinner and could be fatal.

From then on, we ate whole-wheat spaghetti and imitation meat loaf made with soy. Raw sugar or honey in the baking, and kelp to spice food. And for beverages, Mom and Pop juiced everything our garden produced — not just respectable apples or carrots, but beets, alfalfa grass, and watermelon rind.

We kept a large freezer down in our cellar. In the good old days, behind the frozen garden vegetables we kids could always find doughnuts or chocolate-chip cookies hiding. No more.

Once, in the middle of an adolescent growth spurt, after looking down the barrel of raw sugar, I went down there in desperation and opened the freezer. Everything in there was a type of grain. My mom told the story years later of how I stormed up the stairs and revolted. "There is nothing in this house to eat but seeds!" After that she started putting Twinkies in my school lunch. But she kept them hidden so they would last. A little poison to quell a riot.

Now, with all this healthy conditioning, it was high time I started saving my family's life.

The only problem was none of them really wanted me to save their lives. They were perfectly content on the homeschool diet. But it didn't matter. They were going to have long healthy lives even if it killed me.

Of course, all of this would be accomplished within the context of the Faith. We were not going the route of body-beautiful seculars. There had to be a certain spirituality to the way we ate.

And so I come to my next food challenge. Catholicism has a diet all its own. In the Catholicism I grew up with, this presented no more challenge than giving up meat on Fridays and on Ash Wednesday and eating less a mere two days out of every year. "Two small meals that shall not total one full meal" is almost fun.

So, of course, my husband switched to the Eastern Rite. Greek Catholic regulations forbid meat and dairy products on days that pop up often and unexpectedly throughout the liturgical year. Besides this, for the two Sundays preceding Lent — which starts two days earlier than in the West — they start warming you up with Meatfare and Cheesefare Sundays, in which you successively give up meat and cheese. They also throw a two-week fast at you right in midsummer before the Feast of the Assumption. Of course, this doesn't stop the neighbors from throwing steak on the grill.

These are the days we learn gratitude for the abundance in our supermarkets. These are the days that make feasting afterward so sweet. These are the days in which we tell our children these things to keep them from killing us.

For me these days have a charm all their own. Nobody is allowed to get mad if the food doesn't taste good.

∞

It's the End of the (Real)
World as We Know It

Years ago my friend Maria came back to the Church. It was the
end of the world as she knew it.

In her youth, Maria was a heavy-metal fan; born, like a lot of
people in the Sixties, with a deaf wish. But even though rock is
now part of the mainstream, and even though liturgical music had
it goin' on in the Seventies, and even though Bob Dylan did a pa-
pal concert, there is still no Church-sanctioned version of Ozzy.
So she kissed him goodbye.

After that it was goodbye modern TV and movies, goodbye to
certain fashions from Trends R Us, goodbye to checkout-lane
magazines and commerce on Sundays.

She came to me in a moment of despair and asked when it was
all going to stop. When, *when* was life going to seem normal again?

I broke the news: never.

I'm a cradle Catholic who considers being in a coma the only
valid excuse for missing Sunday Mass, and I'm still not done saying
goodbye to the world.

First it was goodbye to electronics, shoes, clothes, and toys
made in Communist China.

Please Don't Drink the Holy Water!

At the same time, there was the Disney boycott. Remember that? It wasn't that their latest princesses were feminists who could "take care of" themselves and routinely rescued men in distress with an agility that was almost cartoonish. It wasn't that Cinderella's and Snow White's torsos had been digitally enhanced for the purpose of advertising. It all fell apart when their subsidiary companies started making movies that brought Catholics out to protest with signs and rosaries.

That was the year the kids got underwear for Christmas.

Then I saw a special on PBS about underwear manufacturers who, in league with the World Bank, are driving third-world nations into insurmountable debt.

An underwear boycott is clearly called for here, but just how long can it go on?

Then there's the problem of eating. Here you are, reading every label to find out what dyes and preservatives are added that might make your offspring sterile in twenty years when you are safely too dead from cancer to file a lawsuit. Naturally you start shopping at health-food stores. On your way in, you see a giant poster of a swami. Great. The store is New Age. Your conscience says there is another health-food store across town. Ten miles. Not far to go to do the right thing. Of course, it is likely that it will also be New Age. You decide to ignore the swami. Where else can you go to get products that look and taste just like the poisonous originals? They cost twice as much, but that's okay. You should really eat less anyway. Thus far, you've got it all worked out. You're proud of yourself.

Then you tell a friend all about it, and she informs you that one hundred percent of the profits from these products go to organizations whose sole mission is to uproot all traces of Christianity from the planet.

It's the End of the (Real) World as We Know It

In a frenzy you run out and buy seeds. Then you shop around in six stores for the best price on a chest freezer.

On your way home, you are exhausted. You pull into a Burger Bits franchise. Your conscience reminds you that you're supposed to be boycotting this one, due to the fact that last year it was an official sponsor of the NAMBLA Olympics. It prods you to go across the highway to the competitor. Just a half-mile down the road, then loop around in the U-turn, a half-mile up again, and ten minutes later you arrive at the competition across the road.

Uh, wait a minute. Maybe *this* is the place you're boycotting, and it's the place you just left that's in the clear. You pull slowly up to the window, trying to ignore the smells seeping into your car. You toy with the idea of asking the cashier if the name Donald Wildmon sets off any buzzers. Right.

You ask yourself, WWJD? That's a tough one. He'd probably opt to go hungry. You ask yourself what would Mom do? No good. She'd be at home, cooking. She never did anything half so frivolous as you just did. You suddenly feel very alone.

The struggle to maintain a standard of Catholic culture is suspended. The smells are too much. You've decided to eat there no matter what. An evil voice inside your head says, "Might as well go all the way. Go on, pull over. Eat it in the car, and while you're at it, blast the radio. The kids will never know. . . . " You pull the burger from the bag and shove it down without allowing yourself to think. You refuse to care whether the franchise serves a cola that funds a charity that donates to an organization that contributes to population control in countries where the World Bank directs unfair labor practices. Perhaps just last week, they switched to a lesser-of-two-evils cola whose only crime is unseemly commercials, but you'll never know. You don't have cable, so you don't get channels that carry unseemly commercials. You can't even tell one cola from another anyway. Besides that, you didn't even get a cola — due to an article you read linking caffeine with premature aging. You are drinking water. Pure, free, chlorinated tap water with added fluoride . . . which has been linked to Alzheimer's . . . in a wax paper cup that makes it taste like blood!

Suddenly none of this matters anymore. You realize you have just eaten a cheeseburger without even unwrapping it.

You leave with a feeling of self-satisfaction you haven't had in a long time. The paper that is now inside you was recycled. You have just done your part in saving the planet!

∞

The TV-Starved Family

It is a well-known fact that a kid who does not watch cable TV is not "up" on the latest trends. This can have an unfortunate isolating effect. Out there in the Real World, if you don't know who the *Friends* are, you might not have any yourself.

Now, I do have a TV. I am not one of those homeschoolers who has completely kicked the habit. Yes, there is a dependency here. I freely admit it, because I know that's the first step toward getting the monster under control. We don't have cable. We keep the set unplugged and covered. Best of all, we have an imaginary lock on it. This lock has prevented the kids from an early age from turning it on or switching channels. Most people who enter our living room do not even know the set is there. Sometimes we forget it ourselves — usually during Advent and Lent.

All this is extremely liberating. But so is knowing in the back of my mind that if the need arises — for example, if I have to do some routine women's work like assembling scaffolding and painting the exterior of the house, undisturbed — the TV's available.

But ah, some might say, the mere presence of the set is a temptation, a near occasion of sin, in fact. Not really. Our program selection consists mainly of bugs mating or Protestant rock videos.

Please Don't Drink the Holy Water!

Both dangerously graphic, I admit, but tempting — not. This is not far from how I was raised. We had a small black-and-white garage-sale deal with two channels and curvy reception. Back in those days, a really entertaining evening consisted of watching the dancers at the Miss America Pageant gyrate to muted sound.

Every year, however, our whole family experiences overwhelming temptation and gives in. We rent a house at the Jersey Shore for a week. The amenities as listed on the place are: garbage disposal, cable TV, dishwasher, iron, TV, deck furniture, smoking, no pets, and TV/VCR. I do not exaggerate. (I mean, at least not at this moment.) The landlord must have known a TV-starved family was coming.

During this period, we take the view that TV-watching, like playing or eating junk food, is part of being on vacation. Besides, a little subculture is an essential part of a complete education, just as a bowl of Sweet Tweets cereal is an essential part of a complete breakfast (which also includes juice, milk, an egg, hash browns, bacon, and toast). Sweet Tweets is the dessert — if you've got room for it. In a cultural diet of Chaucer, Shakespeare, Beethoven, and Michelangelo, we think it is safe to throw in a bit of dessert once in a while.

This year, dessert came in the form of the TV Land network — home of the classic American sitcom. In one week, our kids got fifteen years closer to the Real World. They were already well versed in *Lucy* and *The Honeymooners* (1954), so it was quite a leap to get up to the late Sixties.

The Sixties and the space age sprouted a new kind of TV tree whose branches all fed off the same root: seemingly ordinary people who had a weird but harmless secret that made all the truly ordinary people around them think they were hallucinating; evidence for this is that they frequently rubbed their eyes.

Jeannie: A show I was never allowed to watch as a child because of the skimpy pink outfit. Compared with what's on the beach today, it looks like a habit.

Bewitched: A show I did grow up watching because, although Samantha was a beautiful blonde and did practice the occult, she didn't come across as easy.

Then there's *Mr. Ed,* *The Munsters,* and *The Addams Family.*

Our kids' sitcom level is now holding steady at 1969, where we plan to keep it. The Seventies (*Happy Days, Laverne and Shirley*) have been proven to induce vomiting. The Eighties remind me too much of how I used to dress, and the Nineties — well, maybe by the time the kids are forty, it will look like good clean fun.

Still, if sitcoms have gotten unsafe for children, there is always the Game Show Network. I, for one, consider it a blessed relief that game shows haven't changed in the last fifty years. Vanna White is still alive, and it is still possible for complete morons to win big money. "Name a breed of dog that starts with the letter C." One family got two out of four — chihuahua and chow chow — and won $20,000. Their other answers, "chow mein" and "cheetah," were not on the board. This was an educational experience for the girls. A chance to see America, the land of opportunity, in action. If you can jump high enough and do not object to running around, clutching your head, and screaming in front of a live audience and millions of at-home viewers, you can be a contestant. Hey, it gave them new goals.

Still, Greg and I are choosy about what we let our kids watch. As for ourselves, well, we start out with good intentions. Each year we pledge that, while on vacation, we will control the TV, and each year we fight over who gets to do it. We deceive ourselves, and if that fails, we deceive one another. We tell the other that we will just see what the Weather Channel has to say while we're slathering on the sunscreen before we go down to the beach. But we are TV-challenged, which means we don't know what number the weather channel is. So we flip — all the way to 111. Meanwhile in the blur we have deciphered a half-second of adultery, murder, the dirty secrets of celebrities we've never heard of, and people on top of a jagged cliff pretending to play guitar and mouthing their own songs. But the most mind-boggling had to be Birth TV. I had seen Wedding TV and thought it was the limit of boredom to watch the nuptials of perfect strangers. (I consider my own wedding video a bore.) But Birth TV was worse.

Sentimental music, imperceptible at first, fills the background. The couple's hopes are broadcast in an intimate interview. We accompany them to the ob/gyn, first experiencing weeks of disappointment, only to be with them five minutes later when they finally hear the good news. We progress right along with the pregnancy, making frequent trips to the virtual toilet in the first three months, riding the virtual mood swing, gaining weight right along with them as we reach for more chips. Finally, with ten minutes left in the broadcast, the big day comes. We walk the halls nervously. Then it's into the birthing room for the surprising conclusion: the most intimate moment of all family moments generously shared with the grateful public. Tears, smiles, ecstasy, and an original-sounding name that is guaranteed to belong to at least three others in the kid's kindergarten class complete the show.

It used to be that even husbands were denied access to the mystery. But now anyone with a remote can witness it: children, your parish priest, nuns, the guy who picks up your dry cleaning. And all this, by courtesy of the sponsors, so that some women can shed a virtual tear, sigh a virtual sigh, and spend a real buck.

Cable TV has it tough these days. Like a gangly teenager who has grown too big, too fast, it doesn't know what to do with its power. So many channels, so much air time . . . and there's still nothing on.

Well, almost nothing. Somewhere in the multitude of cable networks you can find a little nun with a big mission. I like to think of her as following the example of her Master, who dined amongst sinners in order to bring them His message. Maybe she'll convert them yet.

∞

Chivalry Is Dead:
It Collided with My Stroller

I never understood why the women of my mom's generation had the urge to roar.

There's something to the old ways, where men and women lived by a set code. Heck, if men would go back to paying for luxuries, opening doors, and fighting for our honor, I could certainly modulate my voice, exude charm, and do a few dishes. It might even be worth wearing a corset.

My mom never roared. She was proud of the fact that she didn't have to support her husband financially. She didn't want her own paycheck. She wanted to spend his. Her name was on at least four store credit cards, and his was on the bills. He didn't seem to mind a bit.

Whose idea was it that we should change this?

It was that class of women who decided to work for eight hours, come home, cook, do housework, and in between drive the kids all over the place, all without a man. And then had the gall to say they were liberated!

Mom felt that she was doing enough. Aside from taking care of a male-dominated household of ten, she taught catechism, counseled unwed mothers, and organized prayer vigils. She never complained about my dad's enormous garden and the acres of farmland that, besides cultivation, provided hours of canning and freezing work for her. She did not complain because she was doing exactly what she wanted to do.

In the early twentieth century, Laura Ingalls Wilder was asked to add her name to the feminist movement. She declined on the grounds of not being able to relate to it. As a farm wife, she knew the priceless value of her economic contribution.

It was the bonbon eaters who wanted out. They were bored and unfulfilled. But I personally blame the men. Once they caught on that they were being let off the hook, there was no stopping it.

Hank: Lois is sick of watching soaps and eating bonbons all day. She wants a job.

Mel: What are you going to do about it?

Hank: I don't know. It'd mean more money, and I'd quit cab driving nights. Course, she'd probably expect me to hang out with the kids more and help with the dishes once in a while.

Mel: Tough choice.

Hank and Mel made up the slogan, "You go, girl!" Hank and Mel are revered by feminists everywhere as sensitive folk-singer types.

Now we have come full circle. Larger household incomes have driven prices up, our material wants have become needs, so now an ordinary paycheck no longer covers the cost of living. Women now get heart disease at the same rate as men, and in a few more years we might yet break even on the mortality rate.

And still, the majority of women will tell you we are better off than our grandmothers were. We can now work on highways and in mail rooms, and at other jobs that were traditionally hogged by men in the past. We can file for divorce just as easily as men and lose custody of our children at the rate men traditionally used to.

To think that in third-world countries with traditional sexual roles, women are missing out on this! The divorce rate is abominably low and the birth rate dangerously high; virginity is prized, and marriage is thought of as a positive good. We must export liberation to these backward places right away!

Even if you manage to stay stubbornly unliberated here, you can't fail to reap the benefits of progress.

For instance, in my sheltered world, my husband carries the baby in one hand and opens doors for me with the other. Out there, in the Real World, doors sometimes drop in my face. Real World logic goes: It's degrading to have someone open a door for a woman as if she can't open it herself. Never mind if she can't because she's pushing a stroller and holding on to a bunch of other kids at the same time. That's the Catholic Church's and her husband's fault for making her have so many children.

Let it be a lesson to all who resist progress!

Still, there is much work to be done. According to some feminists on a talk show I recently saw, the percentage of girls who want to become plumbers when they grow up is still in the negative. Girls still obstinately gravitate toward hairdressing. Everyone knows hairdressers are shamefully underpaid compared with the selfish men who earn three times as much just for unclogging toilets. Remember girls, you're worth it.

Poor mom. She was just too oppressed to know what she was missing.

∞

What's in a Name
(Besides a Royal Title)?

The Bible says that every one of us will have to stand before the awesome judgment seat of Christ and see if our name appears in the Book of Life. The responsibility of all parents, then, is to see to it that their child receives a sensible name. Someday Christ is going to say that name, and it wouldn't do for Him to have trouble pronouncing it.

The standard for naming kids these days seems to be how closely it resembles the names on prime-time soap operas: *Lust in the Dust*, starring Bailey Studson.

TV has really changed America. The current trend in soap-hopeful names has outfitted a whole generation. Yet the closest most of them get is a debut on Court TV: "Kendra Ryder is suing ex-husband Trellis Tiller for the return of a VCR."

These days, if you go by Bill or Mary and an alien ship lands in your bathroom and replaces your toothbrush with a laser that could blow up Los Angeles, you will not be able to find one network that will pick up the story. You will also have trouble finding a single souvenir stand that carries a keychain with your name on it.

Meanwhile, Ryder will be condemned to a life sentence of wrong numbers from people seeking to rent a big yellow truck.

If the Terminator came back to earth to bump off a certain Ashley, he'd have one serious delay.

And poor Sciavone's kindergarten teacher will have to keep referring to his keychain to get the spelling right.

The tendency to bequeath to your kid a name expressive of all your aspirations is nothing new, however. My research shows that it dates all the way back to the Old Testament, when elderly barren matriarchs would finally conceive after a ninety-year novena. Time and again we see Old Testament women getting carried away with joy as they give their sons canticle-size names such as, "God Has Seen Fit to Remove My Reproach from Among Men Thereby Granting Me a Son in Whom Rest All My Newfound Hopes of Never Having to Be Left Out of Another Mothers of Future Patriarchs and Prophets Meeting" (which translates as "Dan").

I always wondered how kids with names like that managed to have normal childhoods. Imagine a neighbor from the next tent down coming to the door. "Mrs. Abraham, can God Has Heard the Cries of His Handmaiden and Granted Me a Son in My Old Age come out to play?"

What does the future hold? Perhaps names like John and Jane will make a comeback in the next generation. It's possible. After all, look what time has done for Zachariah. He no longer conjures up the visage of a hundred-year-old prophet. He's the tattooed teenager in that rock group that practices in the garage across the street.

Meanwhile the generation that begot Bailey will go the way of all mortal flesh — into assisted living — until finally, the day will come when a young nurse named Mary Pat will say, "Wake up, Phoenix honey. We've found your teeth!"

Catholics and Evangelicals are among the last strongholds of social groups that do not name their kids according to the standards of the day. Protestants tend to go biblical — basically

"Mrs. Abraham, can God Has Heard the Cries of His Handmaiden and Granted Me a Son in My Old Age come out to play?"

Please Don't Drink the Holy Water!

because there is nowhere else *to* go when your roster of saint names ends abruptly at the end of Revelation with the word *Amen*.

For Catholics however, the sky's the limit. But this has problems of its own.

"Benedict Francis Pio! You get that cat out of the dishwasher!"

"You just wait till your father comes home, Miss Regina Caeli!"

"Jerome Athanasius, how many times have I told you not to pick your nose?"

"Never interrupt a priest with your mouth full, Thomas Aquinas, and always say, 'Father.' "

By far, the avid papists have the hardest time administering discipline. How can you yell at somebody named John Paul?

I know all this from firsthand experience. The only thing that saved our youngest child from having to live up to the name Campion More was that she was a girl. Anyway, her father didn't go for it. He thought it was too flashy. "We could call him Cam!" I said. "It almost sounds *in*." Forget it. Too out on a limb. So instead he named our tiny child Marie-Bernarde Anne Zita.

There is far too much originality in this world. Everybody is trying to stand out. It starts in the preteens by wearing what everybody else is wearing and carries through to adulthood when helpless offspring arrive just in time for the parents to have used up a sensible supply of dog names such as Grace and Jack.

Does anyone think that the effects might last beyond this generation and the next? What if someday the Pope is forced to raise to the altars a person by the name of Latrina?

∞

B.C.

When our first fruits were in Velcro sneakers, I used to fantasize about how it would be when they grew into shoelaces.

For one thing, I would no longer have to take everybody with me wherever I went. Through a misty golden lens I could picture myself walking through a parking lot with one hand on my purse, the other dangling uselessly at my side. The third had been donated to charity.

Life at home would change, too. The kids would do all the work; they'd babysit while I shopped; they'd homeschool themselves and their younger siblings. My looks would miraculously revert back to twenty-three.

That day is here. I now have babysitters and lawnmowers and receptionists who get rid of telemarketers, and I'm here to tell you that when they say, "Freedom isn't free," they're right.

Right about the time my freedom came in, my image went out.

Let's face it: one of the down sides to your kids growing up is you can't pass yourself off as perfect anymore.

When they were little, our family was classical all the way. I was so cultured, they thought I had studied under Beethoven but given it up to be a stay-home mom. Rock-n-roll was a controlled substance to be taken only when they were napping or far enough from the house to be out of earshot. Two seconds from the first rattle of the doorknob, I could have the radio unplugged and be halfway through whistling the second movement of the Ninth Symphony.

The kids were diehard culture heads. When we walked down the aisle of the supermarket, they'd wince inwardly at the rock-n-roll being piped through the speakers. If they had been fifty years older, they could have been my mother, whose favorite expression was, "Turn off that caterwauling!"

Ah, I was smug in those days. It never occurred to me that one day they would discover I was not what I seemed. That I had been merely impersonating my mother all along — with the skirts, the sensible shoes, the inborn piety.

Mom was a born parent. Having been raised in the decency era, she had an unfair advantage. No matter how my seven siblings and I provoked her, Mom never lost her dignity. It was ingrained.

I cherish the image of her in a house dress and apron. Since I am the last of a large family, many of my friends' mothers were younger. They wore pants, a lot of makeup, and big hair. Some even sunbathed. This was terribly confusing. They didn't *look* like mothers. They couldn't be. They owned the soundtrack from *Hair*. Who knows what other breaches of maternal decency they were capable of?

Smoking?

Mom never even smoked an ordinary cigarette — with or without inhaling.

Cussing?

Once Mom called something "asinine." I was shocked that she would use such language.

Mom was deeply good. In season or out, she never shirked her maternal duty. Grace was part of her.

B.C.

I was born in the late Sixties. That should be excuse enough. Mom was the genuine article. After over fourteen years of mother- hood, I remain but a cheap imitation.

Mom had radar. She could sense when *Love Boat* was on, even in her sleep. As she lay on the couch, I'd inch my fourteen-year-old curiosity closer to the screen and turn down the volume. Twenty minutes into the show, the corny jokes ended and the education began. Just as Doc moved in for another canned love scene (I could never figure out what all those babes saw in him), she'd open one eye. Maybe it was the telltale quiet in the room, or maybe her ears were divinely programmed to pick up saxophone. At a half-slit, the maternal eye saw all. "What are you watching?" was not out of her mouth before all that was left of Doc and a nearsighted trollop was the faint glow of purple light on a blackened screen.

Mom held the Olympic record for lunging from the couch to the off button in mid-sleep — ten feet in .13 seconds.

Pop's standards were the same, but as a man, he had no radar. Female teens can sense this deficiency and are demonically pro- grammed to take advantage of it. I thought I had him in my pocket when once he let me listen to my radio station in the car. The song was a whining, screaming acid-rock tune that I didn't even like. I kept it on only as a matter of precedent. This was going to be the first of many car trips where I would enjoy my music. Dad wouldn't care; he wouldn't even notice.

He put up with it in stony silence for about thirty seconds, then asked deadpan, "What are they saying?" "Uh . . . she's a little run- away. . . . I think." His response was a decisive *click*. He had ways of making me talk. He didn't need radar.

When Greg and I had our first child, our parenting genes magi- cally kicked in. Suddenly everything that our generation had done and gotten away with was baggage, the kind that you shove in the back of the closet and pile things on top of and hope that the kids don't open and have crash down on top of them. There was nothing we could do about it; from then on, we had to be just like our parents.

This would require a bit of revisionist history. First, suppress family secrets such as that Greg's favorite band had been The Who, or that I had once possessed a poster of The Police wearing burned T-shirts and nauseated come-hither expressions.

I consoled myself with the fact that my mom used to subscribe to movie magazines when she was a teen. But that went only so far: her favorite star was Fred MacMurray. It didn't add up to having paid money to be in the company of a screaming, lighter-flicking mob of grass-smokers.

I used to wonder, if I did my Purgatory on earth, could I have such memories burned out of me in time to deny everything — honestly?

I have concluded, through scientific analysis, that the decency gene skips a generation. Our parents had it. Our homeschooled kids have it. My husband and I? Mere carriers.

Our kids have the uncanny ability to say, "Mom!" in the same shocked reproving tone that my mother always used when saying, "Susan!" (If they start saying, "Mother!" that way, I'm running away from home.)

Do they even know what I've suffered for them?

When they were born, I threw away an entire wardrobe. (I couldn't have given it away; that would have been aiding and abetting immodesty.) Turning the stuff into paint rags wouldn't have worked either. The kids would have wondered how we had gotten them in the first place.

Then there were the old photos. What mother worth her table salt would be seen wearing bare shoulders and the arm of a pimply adolescent in a pink cummerbund? I let the kids play with the prom dress only because they assumed it came from a garage sale — that and the fact that it had cost a hundred dollars.

My husband told them I was his only girlfriend and that our first date was when we got married.

We were introduced in a library by an elderly professor who had acted with written permission of my father. We spent our engagement in church and waited a year after we were married to drive alone together in the same car.

I never owned a TV except when *Andy Griffith* was on.

Quarters was another name for tiddlywinks.

I toured Europe with an order of enclosed nuns — saw all the shrines.

Any fun I may have had came from books. My copy of *Canterbury Tales* was edited by Jerry Falwell.

This was life in B.C. (Before Children).

I did all this so that my children would have the same advantage I did. So that someday as grownups they could fondly recall the good old days when my maternal aura formed the backdrop of their childhood.

Then came the fateful day they grew big enough to open the kitchen door without rattling the knob. I dived for the radio plug, but it was too late. There was no use in saying I was waiting for the traffic report; they were on to me. It was in their eyes. If they had been from the previous generation, the next sound would have been *click*.

That was it. I was going on the wagon. From then on, I would have to get my fix in the car. Friends, this is a bad sign. Take it from me: don't rock alone. It means you're no longer just a social rocker, a take-it-or-leave-it rocker, or even a strictly party rocker. You're an addict.

Please Don't Drink the Holy Water!

I started sneaking around. Nine o'clock at night, I'd take the minivan to the dry cleaner. "Be back in ten songs — I mean minutes!" Half a mile from the house it should have been safe to roll down the windows, but the fear of being recognized haunted me.

Then there were the extra trips to the grocery store. This will fool most husbands who haven't stepped foot in one since back when they piped dentist office through the intercom. These days they play a mix of Eighties and Nineties. Their marketing team thinks it encourages spending.

One day a vintage Huey Lewis tune came on. Suddenly I was back in the Eighties. "Cool," I thought. "I was, like seventeen, man, when this first came out." Involuntarily, my feet tapped, hips swayed, head bobbed — you addicts know the look. I glanced at the kids. They were staring at frozen pizza. Then they froze. Our eyes met in the reflection of the half-frosted door. "What are they saying?" they asked. "Uh . . . I want a new drug. . . . I think." They were all thinking the same thing: *click*.

I'd given birth to five mothers.

Part 3

∞

Trust Providence —
Not to Warn You What's Coming

∞

My Other Car Is a Homeschool Bus

Years ago I rebelled against my husband. Before you quote St. Paul at me, hear the facts: a) Greg had insisted on buying a station wagon, and b) we only had one kid.

"Wait a minute," I told him. "A station wagon is supposed to be miles down the road. There's no reason this tiny, immobile child cannot fit neatly into the back of a sports car."

He didn't argue. There wasn't time.

Before I could blink, one child had become two. I blinked again. Two had morphed into three. I blinked again and found that I had given birth to a houseful of their stuff. Numberless dresses, dolls, buggies, plastic dishes, books, blocks, feet-altering Legos, and for the yard, a plastic pool, sandbox, playhouse, and swing set.

After four kids, we traded in the wagon for a seven-passenger minivan. I felt like I was driving a small boat, but in my own way I was resigned.

"That's it!" I told him. "This is where it ends. Minivans are a status symbol. People will think we're in. Just don't ask me to join the ranks of homeschoolers who drive Evangelical-church-size buses."

But it was useless. Every woman knows she has to train her man right from the start — and I had failed. When I had lost the sports car, I lost the war.

By the time we hit five kids, our aging minivan was maxed out. Whenever we took a road trip, the car groaned under the pressure as we packed it with kids, clothes, bedding, indoor toys, beach toys, a folding umbrella and chairs, videos, and groceries. On the outside Greg mounted three bikes on the hatch and used bungee cords to mount three more on the roof rack, first laying a Seventies-vintage orange bedspread underneath to prevent scratching. The only thing needed to complete the picture was a barking hound dog with tongue flapping in the breeze.

All this stress gave our minivan an ulcer; then it slowly bled to a gruesome, oily death. Since we were already at capacity, we reluctantly prepared to buy a full-size.

But once again I resigned myself to the prospect; I was even planning to paint "Lloyds' Domestic Church" on the side of the van, in Spanish. Then we discovered we would need a second income to afford one.

Ite ad Joseph.

St. Joseph has been the patron saint of our material needs ever since we got married and invoked him to keep our rickety dorm-size refrigerator running.

He came through this time in his usual fashion. A mechanic friend had a full-size van that needed adopting into a good home, or else face going to an institution. A 1987, two-tone gray, most of the paint still good, with a decorative hood ornament — an electrical plug sticking through the grille.

Apparently St. Joseph wanted to keep us living in the style to which we were accustomed. And some people don't believe in the power of prayer!

Like a typical man, all Greg cared about was how it ran — which was actually pretty well, once our mechanic friend had gone over it. But since then, the paint has been doing a strip tease, two of the hubcaps rolled away to freedom, and just last week the driver's side mirror dropped down dead. The girls and I feel like the Beverly Hillbillies. Greg? He's perfectly content. The bus runs great and shows every sign of continuing to do so even if the doors should fall off, which I doubt will even then provoke his disloyalty.

I, on the other hand, stare lustily at every young, racy thing we drive past. We've seen several for sale on local highways, but Greg passes by them all, eyes cast down. I guess he really does love the old battle-axe.

I admit it does have a lot of good points. For one thing, I never worry about leaving it alone. Even if I left it unlocked and full of newly purchased Christmas gifts, no one would think to bother it. It can also take a lot of abuse. The sheet metal is so thick, it's virtually undingable. And even if it weren't, it wouldn't matter. I've driven it through tight alleys lined with sprawling shrubbery and not even winced as we scraped our way through the branches. The dent on the roof gives it character. It never demands more than its fair share of rain washings, and its roomy interior is family-fast-food-friendly.

Years of driving sensible old cars had spoiled me, so I really wasn't prepared for what happened next. After years of sharing one family car, my husband finally agreed to a second — and it could be a sports car! We picked out a sleek black convertible. I looked it over, and I couldn't find a thing wrong with it. Shiny paint, a brand-new top, each hubcap present and accounted for, and it was exactly what I had wanted all those years ago — right down to the model year, 1991. Just think how cool I'd look in it — blazing down the highway with my hair lashing my face. Nobody would guess I'm a homeschooler with a closet full of jean skirts. I might even pass myself off as single and liberated.

It was too good to be true.

That was the beginning of a relationship. I have since learned that relationships, while bringing joy, can also make you suffer.

Since we got it, I've named each of the many dings, sighing fatalistically over "Chip," the one that came from an SUV and chipped the paint clean off. I have also nursed it through being sticked (this is like being keyed, but can be buffed back to shine). More recently, when a neighbor boy batted a rock through the windshield and my husband brought me outside to break the news gently, I could only stare, with my shoulders slumped. (What else could I have done? Sports cars are popular targets among vandals. Maybe I should put a bumper sticker on it that reads, "My Other Car Is a Homeschool Bus.") In the meantime, it would have to be fixed. We had come to depend on it, so I would no longer have to drive Greg to and from work every day.

Besides, with his sunglasses on and the top down, he's gotten kind of used to going to work in style. Me? Naturally, I need the van to tote the kids around.

∞

Bless Me, Father

Of all seven sacraments, Confession is the underdog.

Confession, alias Penance, gets nowhere near the hype that other sacraments get. Your parents don't usually throw a party to commemorate your first time. Few even record the date. If you re-member it at all, it's because of the cold sweat you broke into just before your mother pushed you into the close dark box where you were then expected to reveal your most embarrassing secrets, such as that you lied and cheated and hit your siblings.

At some point, the Church decided a new name and a face-lift might help matters. But even though they've been calling it Reconciliation for years now, the embarrassing secrets remain. Until churchmen can figure a way out of that, it is doomed to underpreachment. It's the black sheep of the family.

Perhaps that's why it's my favorite.

Or maybe I like it for the simple reason that I'm a practicing Catholic. Mom always told me that if I kept on practicing, some-day I'd get it right.

I've confessed in boxes, reconciliation rooms, on park benches, and while walking through the Alps; to traditionalists, liberals, and conservatives; to the wise, the mentally ill, the nasty, the sweet, and the understanding. So many different priests have lent me an ear, and God has worked His wonder through them all.

Of these, a few will never be forgotten. Rest his soul, there was the Jesuit of venerable age who once gave me and some women friends an Ignatian retreat. Exercises of this sort often call, not just for a confession, but for a general confession, a recounting of the worst sins of your past life — even those already confessed. The idea is humility. If feeling humiliated is any barometer, I can tell you it works. A half-hour into it, after I had choked on my words and rung out my sleeve, the Jesuit said something to me I'll always remember: "Thank God that during all that time, you never lost your faith." I had never thought of it that way — that no matter what I had done, that much was true. He made me see it as the greatest mercy of my life.

There is one more reason I'm a lifelong fan of the sacrament: there is no greater comedy source in the whole world than what goes on in that sacred box.

As ridiculous as my sins are, the credit does not go to me. My script rarely changes — it's a boring rerun. I quit being shocked and surprised by myself years ago. Besides, I'm the straight man. The priest who plays opposite me gets all the punch lines.

For years I have been confessing to a gentle Polish priest. Again and again, my script called for me to state the horrific ways I have lost patience with my children. Now, this priest happens to know and love our children. So every time I went in there, he tried to encourage me by telling me how wonderful they were turning out. The good man didn't intend it, but this usually led me to re-proach myself even more. What kind of mother would treat "such dear, lovely children" so badly?

Then one day he went on vacation. His substitute was from Po-land, too. His accent was heavy, his voice deep and gravelly. He

growled through my whole recitation. He was building to an erup-
tion, "Don't you come in here and tell me you yell at your kids, you
hit your kids!" He paused to let it sink in. *O God, this is it, I thought.
You're sick of me. I've neglected that firm purpose of amendment for too
long.* Then he blew. "YOU'RE SUPPOSED TO YELL AT THEM
AND HIT THEM!" He was truly exasperated. What kind of
mother was I? Didn't I know my own job?!

Then there's the traditionalist priest who is the best audience
I've ever had. He laughs at everything I say. If your only experience of him was a view of the pulpit, you would think this radically
out of character. His sermons are usually about hell, complete with
graphic descriptions and cliff hangers like, "Where will *you* spend
eternity? The choice is up to you. . . ." And yet, my women friends
say he laughs at them, too. It seems that no matter what we say,
even if it has caused us to cry ourselves to sleep the night before,
this priest can diffuse it. We come out with no choice but to take
ourselves a bit less seriously.

When I was a girl, it was decided that in order to make it more
popular, Confession needed a new look. After the facelift, I barely
recognized it. Light, open space, comfy chairs . . . you wondered
when they were going to bring the cocktails in. Just in case, they
also kept one or two dark, musty boxes around for those of us who
still liked our sins to have atmosphere.

One of the closets I frequented came with more than the usual
brand of privacy. The priest on the other side was stone deaf. Nev-
ertheless he was a fine priest and a gentle one. I can't remember
the number of times he unknowingly interrupted me to ask,
"Those are all your sins, dear?" One time I was still on the number
of weeks since my last confession when he asked, "Those are all
your sins, dear?" I tried over and over to tell him no, I hadn't yet
begun. At one point, I even offered to change places with him as

my side came equipped with a hearing aid. He took my static for a confession and absolved me. On the way home, my parents disputed about whether to send me back in. My mother was pro, my father con.

Besides deafness, this same priest could also be counted on for a mere "three Hail Marys" as penance. Everyone knew this because, due to his hearing problem, he spoke very loudly. One time the majority of our family lined up outside his confessional. As each confession came to an end we heard, "Three Hail Marys," except when it was my dad's turn. For reasons he has never disclosed, he got four.

Later I grew accustomed to the face-to-face method, out of necessity. I was a student in a foreign land. As far as I knew, there was no priest in the vicinity who spoke English but one young man — a fellow student but one who was also endowed with the power to forgive sins. So against a glorious alpine backdrop, God again provided me a way of unloading my sins. I hope they didn't echo.

When I was a student in Rome, it was one size fits all. On a Saturday afternoon I would enter St. Peter's and look for the box that read: Italian, Portuguese, Spanish, and ah, English. As it turned out, the priest inside was from upstate New York, like me. But you wouldn't know it at first. "*In nomine Patris, et Filii, et Spiritus Sancti,*" he grumbled in a thick Italian accent. But he couldn't keep it up. "Hah! Got ya!" he said. He told me his name and asked where I was from. Oh, really? Did I know a priest by the name of Fr. L.? Indeed I did — he was my sister's confessor. "Oh! He's a good friend of mine!" He promised to give me one Hail Mary no matter what. He was the garrulous type, so every Saturday afternoon, we talked for a good half-hour before he handed me my one Hail Mary. To tell the truth, it almost became a deterrent. You were sure to wait in line and then get trapped inside. All this by way of

an excuse to tell you why I was getting more than a little complacent about my sins.

One Saturday afternoon the confessional marked English was
moved. I located it and entered. The priest inside grumbled a
Latin blessing in a thick Italian accent. I waited for him to crack
up. He didn't. For some reason, he didn't seem up to chatting. I
had noticed there was no line. Well and good. I recited my usual
script and waited for my Hail Mary. He then proceeded to give me
a guided tour of my place in hell. Any minute now, I figured, he is
going to crack up and give me a Hail Mary, but he never did. Just
who that was on the other side of that cubicle I'll never know, but I
went straight from then on.

So many confessions, so many years. I've lost count of them,
but the highlights will never be forgotten. You can always tell a
Catholic by the way he sits up when the subject of Confession is
mentioned. We've all got our stories.

∞

Do-It-All-By-Yourself

Thrift was the dominant trait in both my parents.

With eight children to share the load, do-it-yourselfing was a way of life in my family. When I say way of life, I'm not exaggerating. Once my parents even unscrewed and dragged the toilet out into the backyard to fix it. Servicemen were like the Tooth Fairy to us. We never saw one, but other kids swore they existed.

This turned out be a boon to my later life. You see, we have an old house. Since moving in thirteen years ago, Greg and I have replaced the flooring, the roof, the paint, the paper, drywall, windows, doors, some plumbing and wiring, cabinets, some major appliances, and a large portion of the foundation — which was kind of sad, because it had faithfully served several generations of termites. In spite of this, the house still shows signs of going on one hundred.

So do I. I married an intellectual.

Before I met Greg, I asked St. Joseph to find me a guy like himself. I was thinking along the lines of godly, kind, strong, and industrious. He delivered Greg, who besides all of the above, was cute.

But I was young. Young and inexperienced. It never occurred to me to ask St. Joseph, the patron saint of handymen, for a guy with sawdust flowing through his veins.

Please Don't Drink the Holy Water!

At first it didn't worry me. Like my mom, I had chosen brain. Greg was a guy with talent. He could speak two foreign languages fluently and fake four others, had been a Fulbright scholar, and was a born workaholic. Plus, we lacked money. All this no doubt would come together at the necessary time. . . .

Then one day my brother, a carpenter (and chip off the old oak block), shipped us a set of cabinet door and drawer fronts, which Greg pledged to reface and install.

The box was planted in the middle of the kitchen floor and stayed there so long that it evolved into a kitchen island. We chopped vegetables on it, wrote emergency telephone numbers on it, and served from it when there was company. Later, when we finally moved it, the tiles underneath were a different color.

The problem was not Greg. He's perfectly willing to learn new things, and his work is always meticulously done. The problem was the lack of Greg.

When you run a nonprofit, as he does, your mind is always at the office; and more often than not, so's your body. The chosen patron for this line of employment is known as Our Lady of Perpetual Work.

I tried nagging; I tried begging. Finally I threatened to take out an ad in the paper:

Wanted: Husband. Must Work for Food.

I didn't want a new husband, mind you. I just wanted to borrow somebody's old one for a while. Greg advised against it. He thought people might get the wrong idea.

Now, due to heredity and environment, some would say I am determined to have certain expectations of a man. You can't blame me for this. On top of this, there is the simple fact that most women, by nature, find men most attractive when they are wearing sweaty old clothes and carrying a tool box.

This feminine do-it-yourself instinct originated in prehistoric times when there were no checking accounts, no investments, and no artificial wealth, which men today use to impress their prospective mates. Only rudimentary tools and the bare, capable hands of the caveman could elicit that certain look of rapt admiration in a cavewoman. It dates all the way back to the first cave apartment and is probably responsible for the priceless prehistoric cave art in museums today.

Cavewife (looking around in disgust): "You know what these walls could really use? Some pictures of buffalo or elk or whatever you call those things we had for dinner last night. Just sort of running or leaping. That would really perk the place up."

Now, what the cavehusband says in response shows whether, at this point in prehistory, the saying "Happy wife, happy life" has been chiseled somewhere.

If he says, "Hulga, this sort of project will someday be proven by archaeologists to have taken several decades. It's not like there are any paint stores around yet. I mean, I'd have to gather herbs and probably boil them. Do you know how many herbs that would take? I'm not even sure of what kind to use, and well, fire is not my specialty either. Maybe Grunt down in the next cave could come in and do it. He's good with fire at least. Then again, he's pretty busy. It might be a while. But since you've got your heart set on it, tell you what: I'll ask Grunt for some pointers and we'll go from there. . . ." — then the little woman will inform him that if he won't do it himself, he shouldn't complain if she pays Grunt however many skins of nameless beasts he asks to get the job done.

His response to that would probably be to ignore it and hope that this means that the subject is closed and that she'll just forget about it. But we who have the benefit of a historical standpoint all know that he will never hear the end of it.

Please Don't Drink the Holy Water!

His best bet, even if he doesn't have a clue about fire or herbs or even what kind of beast they had for dinner last night, will be to show his wife some enthusiasm. He is going to end up with the job anyway, so he may as well save himself a lot of stress and time. He could start gathering twigs and cutting off locks of his hair. He could let his wife see him binding the twigs and hair together. If she catches him sitting still, he could say that he was just turning over in his mind whether the leaping beasts should have horns or antlers. After all, you have to do these home projects right.

By and by, he will paint something resembling a beast leaping, and she will invite her friends in to see it, and they will want their husbands to do the same for them, and this pattern will continue until, one day, millions of years later, a male and female Home Depot will evolve simultaneously and reproduce all over the planet.

Now, like me and the above ancestors, Greg, too, had expectations when he married me. Since I was a fellow philosophy student, the idea of my demanding that he wake up early on a Saturday morning so that I could stare at him in ecstasy as he put on sweaty old clothes never entered his mind. Besides, he came from a household that ran on the biblically sound distribution-of-labor system, where servicemen were known by their nicknames and thought of as old friends.

Greg's projects always start the same way. I ask him for a Saturday. He gets out his planner, and there's nothing available for three months. I am a desperate woman. I take it.

The day arrives. Greg is hiding something. . . . He comes clean. He has to do urgent office-related errands first. But don't worry. It will just take up the morning.

He gets back by about 2 p.m. Yes, yes, he knows he's two hours late, but he happened to run into someone who needed converting. Cabinets can wait, but salvation can't.

He assures me, the rest of the day is mine . . . as soon as he has a bite to eat. After that he just has to make one phone call. He wants to invite the recovering apostate over for dinner. No, not today, no fear. Today he promised he would start the cabinets. He will, most faithfully, start them.

By quarter to four, he is ready to begin. Right after Confession.

I argue that the day is already far spent. After that, why bother? He agrees and commends me for being so reasonable.

As a last, desperate resort, I hold up a legal contract, signed in blood, stating that he will start the cabinets that day. He concedes defeat.

By 8:30 p.m., he has the box open. By ten, the doors are stacked nakedly where the box was.

With the help of a sympathetic brother (his own this time), Greg did get the cabinets up within a few weeks. And I must admit they look great. But I had learned my lesson. On that night when I threw the empty box by the curb, I made sure to copy all the phone numbers off it first.

One of them belongs to a handyman.

∞

A Little Wet Chocolate

I'll never forget the moment I knew that Greg was the man I would marry. He was what we girls used to call "marriage material," a good Catholic, educated, handsome, and embarrassingly gallant. But for me, the decisive moment came when I saw him eyeing his two-year-old niece's chocolate Tastycake. It was dangling halfway out of her mouth along with enough drool to wash it down. Finally she had had enough. She threw it across the table, landing it right in front of Greg. "O sweetheart," he admonished, "you can't waste that!" Then he popped it into his mouth.

Disgusting, hilarious, and inspiring. Right then I knew that Greg would make our future kids a great dad.

Perhaps I'm the first girl to give my heart to a guy because he eats soggy chocolate. But I'm not the first to know the value of a father's love.

In *The Story of a Soul*, the Little Flower recounts that she met God the Father through her own dad. It was as simple as going fishing and taking long walks in the countryside together. The Church has already recognized the greatness of this ordinary man (and his wife) by naming him Venerable. To Greg and me, his greatest achievement was to give each one of his five daughters in marriage to Christ Himself. Since we also have five daughters, we hope to see Venerable Louis Martin named as the patron saint of the Prevention of Expensive Weddings — if such a thing could be translated into Latin.

Like Venerable Louis, my husband also loves to spend time with his girls. Being from a male-dominated household, he jokes that God must have sent girls to civilize him. Our closets are bursting with dolls, not one of which has an arrow stuck in it. Greg's favorite form of recreation, a hike up a craggy bluff, has devolved into a meandering stroll through the woods, with a toddler instead of a rucksack on his back. His vacation of choice, touring Civil War battlefields, rarely gets an enthusiastic response unless it includes shopping for vintage bonnets afterwards. And to his mother's delight, he is frequently encouraged to take a shower, although it isn't always possible to get an appointment.

Somehow girls are born knowing that they're the boss. One time Greg lay on the living room floor with Miss Toddler propped up on his knees playing a game that goes, "I saw a fox last night. What color was it?" Miss Toddler was supposed to try different colors until she guessed the color he was thinking of, then his knees would go apart and send her crashing down. This was great fun until Miss Toddler correctly guessed brown. Instead of giggling when she came crashing to the floor, she objected, "No, *pink!*"

Once in a while, though, the girls let Greg play a guy game: war on our living-room "battlefield." It's always the French versus the English. Greg plays the English — no small sacrifice for an Irishman — and invariably St. Joan's forces trounce him. I stay on the sidelines to care for the wounded and count bodies. The battles usually end when one of the girls bursts into tears because the others are "hurting Daddy!" He shows them, of course, that they haven't really made a dent. Gathering them to himself, he lets them climb up his legs and hang off his arms like George Bailey in "It's a Wonderful Life," when he got back from not being born.

Unlike George, however, Greg has never wished his children away. At the birth of our fifth non-boy, more than one member of H.R.u.M.F. attempted to offer condolences. His reply was a laughing, "Blessed am I among women!" Maybe Venerable Louis said the same when his wife gave birth to their fifth non-boy, St. Thérèse.

Greg claims that our lack of a son with whom to share his guy interests doesn't bother him in the least. Not in the least, I assure you. He's perfectly happy with the present arrangement, he says to tell you. While I'm sure he would continue to maintain this even if we were to have five more girls, I can't help but notice the way he acts around our friends' sons. Suddenly Greg senses he is among his own pack. His ears perk up like a dog getting ready to chase a speeding car. He greets the kid by grunting his name. (When he speaks to girls, it's always "sweetheart" or "angel.") Friendly insults are exchanged, followed by pushing, shoving, and noogies. All of this is guy-code for affection. I learned this when I had a chance to observe Greg's relationship with his older brother Paul. Nothing pleases him more than when Paul pounds on him and threatens to beat him up. It's quite moving, actually.

"Blessed am I among women." Perhaps with a little luck and a lot of grace, one of our daughters will carry on the family name the way little Thérèse Martin did.

~

The Case of the Supplanted Sibling

Did you ever pick up a parenting magazine? You know the sort I mean. You find them in grocery stores, at your ob/gyn, and any-where else that is likely to attract mothers. These are in a class by themselves: the only magazines in the world that try to limit the growth of their potential readership. First, they hook you by the cover, where you see a baby so gorgeous, it's edible. So you open it. Then, instead of being told where to get one, you see ads and arti-cles dedicated to the suppression of future offspring.

How this boosts subscriptions now and in the future I can't fig-ure. Nor do I understand why doctors' offices litter their waiting rooms with this stuff.

Then, there's the treatment of existing kids. Here you find arti-cles like "Breaking the News: Helping Older Kids Adjust to a New Baby." Once the dreaded baby arrives, parents are urged to "spend time one-on-one with the older child. Make a point of putting the baby down and letting the older child sit on your lap. Tell the older child he is important, that you have room in your heart for him, too." (Please note, use of the word *he* by no means implies that said child is male. These magazines are up-to-date on the lat-est regulations from the Committee for Rights Among Pronouns, which specifies that the use of the word *he* will alternate every other paragraph with *she*.) All of this allegedly staves off fear and envy. If that fails, please turn to the advertising section for a complete list of reassuring gifts for the dethroned sibling.

Now, I'm no licensed psychologist, but I do have five kids. I know something about how demanding and selfish children can be. Right now, ours are demanding a new baby.

They're becoming a bit dissatisfied with the old one. Oh, they will acknowledge that she's even cuter than the day we got her and that, as toddlers go, is in excellent general working condition. It's just that she has developed a thing called "a mind of her own." While somewhat charming, it does come with preferences, tantrums, and obstinacy. This means she won't always allow herself to be treated like a baby. She won't often be rocked, she won't always kiss and hug on demand, and the mechanism that makes her stay in the same place you left her in is broken. Instead, she is usually in their room getting into their stuff.

They've voiced their demands to their father and me. We've told them we would be happy to provide a baby for them, but that the matter lies in God's hands. Since then, they've been praying every night.

Jealousy? Yes, they are jealous of everybody we know who has a baby.

If God does send another one, they have already claimed it as *their* baby. I will be permitted to handle it only if I take proper care of it. I'll never forget the first time I slapped our youngest's hand as she was going for the electrical outlet. The other four girls leapt to her defense. They nearly laid hands on me. I had made *their* baby cry! Who did I think I was?

What about the littlest one? Sure, the older kids might want a new baby but how does the reigning queen feel about it?

The Case of the Supplanted Sibling

I've been through a baby regime change four times, and every time, the reigning queen was just delighted to hand down her crown. Our first child was so excited, she acted as if she was telling me something I didn't know. "Mommy! Baby!" she exclaimed, pointing to the cradle. Her first sentences were almost all baby-centered: "Baby cries." "Baby sneeze." "Baby poo-poo."

She was not yet two then. The last time it happened, the queen was four and a half years old, so I wasn't sure how she would react. She had been a popular queen. She had had her picture taken so often, she was nearly blind. Not long after her baby sister's arrival, she went over to her and cuddled her in her arms. She looked up at me, beamed, and said, "This would be a good time to take a picture." It never hit her that she was out of a job. I took the picture.

Just out of curiosity, the girls asked their current baby sister how she would feel about having a new baby around. She cooed and talked in a baby voice just as she does when mothering her dolls. She seems to like the idea.

Wait a minute. . . . This is not how things are in the Real World! Perhaps I should sit her on my lap and read *Nobody Asked Me if I Wanted a Baby*! Then maybe she'd respond with the appropriate degree of fear and malice.

After Greg and I tell them a new baby is expected, we all thank God together as a family. (Unlike some people in the Real World, we do not take credit for "making" our babies. I can barely make curtains.) During the nine months that follow, we continue to pray for the little one and to let the other kids participate in every way they can.

During my last pregnancy, the four girls and I sat on our big bed, rifling through the hand-me-downs like old ladies at a rummage sale. Each rumpled outfit had its own story, complete with illustrations (stains). We put a tiny sock on the end of a pencil and a sweater on a doll, and I told stories about them as infants. The juicier, the better. Literally. Spitting up, belching in church, and squirting mustard doo all over Grandma at bath time were big hits. Instead of feeling like outsiders, each one got a glimpse of her own advent. Each one learned that it was our love for her that made us desire more children.

Somewhere in the middle of all these preparations, it occurred to the kids that they wanted to give something to the baby — something just from them. After all, what's a birthday without presents? They got out their sewing needles and glue and came up with a doll, a bib and a set of felt/cardboard booties with glitter. Someday she'll be old enough to read the message hidden in each of these: "We loved you even before you were born."

During my last two weeks of pregnancy, I had a throbbing blue leg, insomnia, and a distinctive waddle. But the kids were more restless than I was. Somehow they got the idea that babies come in the middle of the night. Every night they went to bed excited, and every morning I opened one eye to find a dejected face staring down at me. "She's still here!" the designated reporter would announce. When the night finally came that I did have to depart for the hospital, the kids sounded off like the stroke of midnight on New Year's Eve. I doubt that scene would have played the same if we had prepped them for the baby by telling them, "Don't worry. We'll still feed you."

When they finally got to meet their baby the next morning, they asked for no other gift but the privilege of holding her in their arms. For a moment, jealousy made its only appearance. Each one wanted to go first.

∞

Blessings in Disguise

Having five girls has brought one problem: people keep asking if we are "trying for a boy."

My husband has been consoled numerous times. One old lady at church remarked sadly, "Well, as long as it's healthy, right?" Anyone would agree this is a perfectly natural response to the sight of a shining white infant, freshly born again on the day of her Baptism.

The fact that my husband and I have never expressed a desire to determine our children's sex is irrelevant. In our view, not getting "lucky," or "missing out on the chance of having a boy" are remarks consigned to the Incomplete category, like the nebulous place they come from called the "Real World."

It's the same with the recurring remarks some of us face about family size.

"Are you done?" "So is this it for you?" "Don't you have a TV?"

These remarks used to make me angry, but now they crack me up. People never fail to think they are being original.

Most of us idealize family size in accordance with what we're used to. My parents were Uber-Catholics; they had eight children. Below four is small in circles where you don't hit supersize until you go nine and up. Now, we ourselves are currently maintaining five, which means we are experiencing the mid-size crisis.

In the Real World, it just doesn't make sense for educated persons living in a progressive society to have that many children unless we were holding out for that elusive boy. (Where feminism suddenly went I'll never know.)

On the flip side, we are far from reaching supersize proportions. As other people have hinted, five is not terribly sacrificial. We could be doing better.

And so, there it is. We just don't fit in. So I've decided to join the ranks of those who, while maintaining that it's none of the Pope's business, proceed to explain and justify their family plan to every other person on the planet.

Drum roll please. . . .

The top ten blessings in disguise about having a middle-size family made up entirely of girl children:

10. There is not one single person in my family I cannot walk in on in the bathroom.

9. Greg has never had to do toddler potty duty in public places.

8. Girls remember birthdays, anniversaries, and Mother's Days, and they make sure my husband does, too.

7. Greg gets the harem he always wanted without having to change religions.

6. When the doorbell rings, the house undergoes a complete renovation in ten seconds.

5. Organized revolt is impossible. Tower of Babel Syndrome makes all team efforts result in communication breakdown.

4. Toys, clothing, decor, Halloween costumes, and extracurricular activities are all recyclable.

3. Our funerals will be well-attended.

2. They actually want to see our wedding video.

And number one:

Not only do we have fast, reliable, and clean-cut help; they have reached the age where they wonder how we ever got along without them.

So do Greg and I. We can't imagine life any other way. When we look at our wedding pictures, we expect them to be there. When we reunite with an old friend, we expect them to call him "uncle." Maybe it's because they are the children God intended us to have from all eternity.

"Just Wait Until They're Teenagers!"

There are no guarantees, you know.

I sat there with half my hair pulled through the plastic silver cap, looking like an alien out of a Sixties B-movie. The idea was to get red highlights, but I knew that one false move could turn me into Lucille Ball. The hairdresser squinted at me from the mirror, her gloved hands waving the sharp plastic hook that would determine my do's destiny. I was a victim waiting to dye. So I didn't dare argue with her.

For she had just pronounced sentence: "Just wait until they're teenagers!" What could I say to that? Her kids were putting her through hell. The closest I had come to child-inflicted Purgatory was an afternoon at Chuck E. Cheese's.

Besides, I had met parents like her before. She had all the marks of a member of H.R.u.M.F. (the club for Hairdressers, Relatives, *und* Malfunctioning Friends) whose mission is to scare homeschoolers and other Catholic parents who might make the fatal mistake of trying too hard. So I knew it was senseless to argue. And, of course, she might end up being right. The fact that our kids were well behaved in their youth was no guarantee they'd stay that way.

I filed the warning away in my official Gloomy Predictions folder. It was not alone there.

Prediction number one came when we got engaged. It went, "Don't get married. You don't know what you're letting yourself in for." This advice came from people who were divorced and seeking a relationship.

I remember attempting to argue that Greg and I didn't believe in divorce, and that we were relying on God's help. "Hah! That's no guarantee!" came the triumphant answer — which is, of course, true, because you always have to factor in fallen nature. Anything can happen. I mean, what if one or both of us suddenly became internationally handsome and had millions of fans chasing after us and was not able to resist the temptation? Naturally, even the resolve of a saint would crumble.

The second gloomy prediction arrived at the same time the first child did. It went, "You may be against contraception now, but when you have too many kids, you'll change your mind." That was five kids ago. Granted, that's not as many as some Catholic families have. Maybe if five more come, rebellion will set in. There's always hope.

In our case, the "we're done" announcement, which is usually delivered to a chorus of friends, relatives, and perfect-strangers-you-meet-by-chance-in-line-at-the-grocery-store, would rather go something like this:

Us: Ladies, Gentlemen, and Perfect Strangers, we'd like to announce that we're done. Please, don't get up and leave the room. We don't mean to make you uncomfortable that we are bringing up such a personal subject, but it's been on our consciences. Please give a sign of validation.

Chorus: Well, it's about time! You've got ten grandchildren!

"Just Wait Until They're Teenagers!"

Then when we started homeschooling, a whole family of gloomy predictions moved in like poor relations — to stay. They said:

"If you shelter your children from *everything*, they will never learn to function in the Real World."

"What if your daughter delays rebellion until she's nineteen and has a car?"

"What if you miss something and your kid goes on *Jeopardy* and doesn't know the question?"

It has finally dawned on me that these challenges are a form of popular entertainment. You win the game when you get to see your friends gnashing their teeth on the six o'clock news. It seems that there is nothing more fun than a good disaster.

Now, I have nothing against disasters per se. We did our part during the Y2K scare. Greg bought two kerosene lamps and I, a gallon of water. After that we lost interest. If Armageddon had come, there would have been plenty of light for the mourners to keep vigil over our dehydrated, grubby remains.

Friends of ours were much better prepared. They bought an entire harvest of flour, dug their own well, got a huge dog and a Waco's worth of ammunition. Guess where we spent New Year's Eve? The morning after dawned bright and crisp, giving no outward sign of the bizarre let-down feeling that enveloped all of us.

With that flurry long over, there is always reality TV. Now, we are terribly cultured in our house. We do not lower ourselves to watch network reality-TV shows, nor does network TV even make an appearance in our house — except on a really clear day if we take turns holding the rabbit ears and leaning on the set. Luckily, PBS offers its own version of survival for sadists to the culturally elite: *1900 House, Frontier House, Manor House,* and *Colonial House,* the shows in which ordinary stupid people volunteer to live in grueling conditions for three months, to prove that . . .

they can? Cheating sets in, marriages break up, people gossip about their neighbors into a hidden camera and, in general, barely stave off nervous breakdowns. The shows are a hit. Maybe PBS should consider:

Homeschool House

The Challenge: To take an ordinary family, place them in a contrived Real World homeschool situation, bar all doors and windows, and watch them kill themselves. Sponsored by contributions from viewers like H.R.u.M.F.

My mom used to say she'd be judged on her children's behavior. There were eight whom she brought into this world and nurtured with loving hands. If at times we failed to meet industry standard, it certainly wasn't because she didn't try. Judgment Day has already come for her good soul. She could stand before the Lord with gray hairs in hand and say, "No matter what people said, I believed in You and I never gave up."

And I can tell you, no matter what she suffered, she never wished it on another soul.

∞

What Kind of Mother Are You?

Not just for homeschoolers but anyone who communicates in terms of A, B, and C.

Child rearing is a fulfilling and satisfying time of a woman's life. It is also a busy one. Whether it's homemaking, homeschooling, home remedies, home birth, or home orthodontia, it seems we just never have enough time to reflect . . . on ourselves, our families, and our communities.

This easy quiz will help you record your progress during this hectic time of life. Circle the one that best describes you, and then add up your points to see what you've won. Give yourself one point for each A, two points for each B, and three points for each C.

1. APOSTOLIC ZEAL
You are seen pregnant in public with three children or more. A stranger asks if they are all yours and if you're done. You . . .
A. Say with edification, "I will gladly take as many as God sends."
B. Say with annoyance, " 'Scuse me, do I know you?"
C. Point to your belly and say, "All but this one."

2. AMBITION
You secretly view your children as potentially . . .
- A. Becoming saints.
- B. Becoming a reflection of your own undiscovered genius and waning beauty.
- C. Becoming wealthy enough to support you someday in a style to which you are not accustomed.

3. MODESTY
One evening you put your favorite little skirt on a hanger, and the next morning . . .
- A. You start a diet so that next time it won't be so snug.
- B. Your husband has dressed the toddler in it to make a point.
- C. It has gained eight inches and turned denim.

4. CHARITY
A teenager stops you on your way out of Cheepomart and asks you to put some spare change in his plastic bucket to help finance a class trip to Italy. Your response is to . . .
- A. Inform him that his entire education is already on you, as a taxpayer, while you have to beg the government for a lousy tax credit to buy textbooks for your own kids.
- B. Tell him that in your day spare change was used to buy a plastic bucket to go wash cars and *earn* the money.
- C. Throw in five bucks to stave off guilt and to avoid a confrontation.

5. EFFICIENCY
You have a friend who complains that she is way behind on the housecleaning. You exhort her to . . .
- A. Train her kids to help out.

    B. Invite people over — a sure way to get the cleaning done.

    C. Lower her standards.

6. UNSELFISHNESS

Another friend complains that her family eats up the groceries as fast as she can buy them. You assure her that . . .

    A. All families need to eat.

    B. The sacrifices she is making running to and from the store are being recorded in heaven.

    C. You view a full pantry as merely decorative.

7. DISCIPLINE

You believe the goal of discipline is to . . .

    A. Train your children in Christian virtue.

    B. Teach them social skills so they can make it in the Real World.

    C. Get them from one end of a department store to the other without having to crawl under the clothing racks.

8. JOB SATISFACTION

You know your kids are growing up when . . .

    A. They start taking responsibility for themselves and planning their future.

    B. They show maturity by talking like you to their younger siblings.

    C. They ask if you've called ahead, locked up, have your keys, and have done you the courtesy of pinning your gloves to your sleeves.

9. ENERGY

The method of punishment you use most often is . . .

    A. Chase a kid down and then administer a spanking.

    B. Yell and flail your arms from the couch.

    C. Say nothing, but pounce on them when they least expect it and wilt them with the Mr. Spock nerve pinch.

10. EXPERIENCE

You have been invited to a baby shower. You bring . . .

    A. A cute little outfit with matching booties that the kid will grow out of in two weeks.

    B. A stuffed animal to add to the ark.

    C. A plastic barf bucket containing disinfectant, bleach, rubber gloves, and disposable cleaning cloths.

11. SPOUSAL CONCERN

Your husband has had a long day at the job. You make sure he . . .

    A. Eats a hot meal and takes a nap.

    B. Eats quickly enough so that he still has time for chores before dark.

    C. Notices you working to impress on him that there are four hours left to your workday.

12. ANXIETY FACTOR

You consider a really bad day to be when . . .

    A. Armageddon happens.

    B. The Three Days of Darkness happen.

    C. The toddler learns how to work the bathroom doorknob.

Your score:

12-18 points: While you undoubtedly deserve a perfect score, we wouldn't want to ruin your chances of getting your reward in heaven by giving it to you down here. Besides, we couldn't possibly compete in the prize department.

19-28 points: Your reward is sympathy. You are still trying desperately to maintain standards and have not given up hope. Besides this, you use expressions like, "in my day" which, let's face it, is something your grandmother used to say.

29-36 points: We have nothing to offer you, but you don't need us anyway. You are on your way to winning perseverance, which is more valuable to the Catholic soul than all the art treasures in the Vatican.

∞

Father Necessity

It has always been a source of embarrassment to me that I don't take after my father more. Under normal circumstances — meaning scratch out homeschooling — it would be quite sufficient that I should take after my mother. She had all the right qualities for her vocation of wife and mother.

For one thing, common sense flowed from her like water. For another, she was organized and dutiful. Her intellectual bent was toward the humanities, theology, music, politics, history, and literature. All this was topped with a strong moral code that brooked no nonsense, none of the time. When I grow up, I hope to be just like her.

Under the abnormal conditions of homeschooling, this is a fine start. However, it would come in handy if I had just a fraction (whatever that is) of my dad's talent for math and science.

Pop grew up on a prosperous farm in Maine and then put himself through the university. As an aside he took up flying because it was fun and an efficient way to travel. He could grow anything, build anything, and fix anything. He invented things, too — like the water distiller he made while resting up after a heart attack. With lengths of copper tubing, a heating and cooling device made from get-well cards and a fish-tank motor, it took up half the kitchen and dripped at a rate of one drop per five seconds — but it worked.

My mother took this sort of thing for granted. She hailed from Maine, too. Everyone knows that the dominant gene running through New Englanders is thrift. Far from being overly impressed, she used to throw a blanket over the distiller whenever the doorbell rang.

Although we lived in the suburbs where neighbors planted in-ground pools, the flat of our yard (a large sunny expanse that any child could see was designed by God from all eternity for a pool) housed a massive garden. In addition we had around sixty-five acres about forty miles outside of town, on which we grew crops. Yes, crops, such as corn and potatoes and row upon row of carrots, beans, and peas. Why, I don't know. We didn't go to market with these crops, and we wouldn't have been able to give them away fast enough even if we had dropped them into open car windows at the mall. What we couldn't eat fresh, my mother canned, froze, and pickled. To us children, it seemed that our parents' main use for planting crops was to create work. In reality, it was probably a combination of my father's urge to get back to the farm and my mother's belief in the immanence of the Three Days of Darkness.

On this land Pop and my brothers erected a barn. They painted it red. They parked the big tractor in it. At the top of a distant hill and into a shady forest was a spring. On every visit, my mom and I trudged up and filled jugs with rich, earthy spring water, then slogged our way back down like pack mules. This got old fast, even to Mom. So Pop got himself a mile of copper tubing, dug a shallow channel, and erected a tap in front of the barn. There we could fill the jugs just by turning on the spring.

This was in his spare time.

For his day job, Pop was an aerospace engineer. He designed space clocks for GE under government contracts. His work was highly classified. If there had been a take-your-daughter-to-work day back then, I wouldn't have been allowed in. Of course, not all of his work was done in his head. He leaned heavily on the technology of the day: slide rule and graph paper.

The construction of my brain was nothing like this. I had been bewildered by math and science since third grade. My mother tried to be encouraging: "Pop's the smart one. You take after me." Mom had a bad habit of selling herself short, so she didn't realize the effect it would have on me — which was to cement my suspicion that I was hopelessly addled from birth.

Even so, this might have been fine except that the school I attended stubbornly refused to consider any child a hopeless case. They persisted in giving me homework and expecting me to master material for tests. The natural place to go for help was to Pop. Night after night, we played the near-strangulation scene.

"I think I'm starting to get it, Pop," I'd say, nodding and squinting for effect, after he did my first two algebra problems to show me the method. "It's still a little fuzzy in spots, though."

He'd breath deeply in a noble effort to control himself, then do two more. Then the dreaded words, "Now you try one."

"There's only one small thing I don't get: how you can add letters and end up with a number. . . . "

He'd do another. This time the instructions were louder.

Once the lessons reached the decibel level where kids from the neighborhood at large could have benefitted from my tutoring, I'd end the scene by pretending to get it and just needing some time alone with it. Pop would recede into a semi-lit room to sip a beer and forget, while I'd make a mental note to volunteer the answer for one of the first five problems at school the next day.

These sessions were not a total loss, however. Pop no doubt grew in patience and virtue, and I discovered I had acting talent.

I passed algebra. I didn't learn anything, but I passed fair and square (whatever that is). My teacher, Mrs. M., was a kindly woman who gave up much of her time for my sake and the sakes of many others who did not take after their fathers. She wouldn't have dreamed of threatening me with the last laugh, but she got it anyway. Now that I have a highschooler of my own, there is no way out. I have to learn algebra. There are four kids in the lineup after this one. Not only that. Besides cramming the dreaded material into my own head, I am faced with teaching someone who has about the same level of affection for algebra that I once had. (Mrs. M., if you're out there — HA!)

The egalitarian philosophy of the school also meant that cruel and unusual punishment known as the annual science fair. Just in case you weren't embarrassed enough among your classmates, you had to present something of your own making in front of the whole student body, plus their parents. (Not to mention your own, the very same people who are paying hundreds of dollars for your tuition.)

Some kids reveled in it. You know the type. The kid with the mini-Vesuvius who, at the touch of two wires — *blammo!* A cloud of pink smoke rises, and it erupts in flowing lava, destroying scale-replicas of Pompeii and Herculaneum. The kid has also figured out how to get it to do this more than once for the purposes of demonstration.

Then there's the cow's-eyeball-floating-in-the-glass kid. Now, what kind of sick, resourceful child knows where to procure such an object? An obliging local farmer? A mail-order catalog? Nobody else knows. Only one thing is certain. He passed.

Then there was my project: a Twanger. It was a flat piece of painted wood with two nails hammered into each side and two rubber bands stretched across the middle. When you plucked the rubber bands, it was supposed to go *twang*. But I couldn't even get it to do that. It went *flunk*. So I showed it to Pop. By the time he was done rebuilding it with pegs and guitar strings, it went *twang*. A solid C. Not the note, my grade.

Now that I am grown and am free from the threat of displaying my ignorance at science fairs, I find science fascinating. I am the sort of person who finds nothing more enjoyable than a good volcano demonstration. I would frequent the Air and Space Museum if it were convenient. My idea of a good TV show is *Nova*.

I'll go further than that. I miss my dad's farm. Although we kids unaffectionately dubbed it "the Lot," I now feel proud to have been part of it.

But I have my limits. I refuse to have a lab in my home.

I burn myself too easily as it is. I am also not well-stocked in "basic household ingredients" of the kind that kit-makers think everybody has on the shelf, like magma or plutonium. Whenever I dream about hell, the atmospheric smells of formaldehyde and fetal pig parts are sure to be somewhere in the background. I see no benefit to the years I spent carving up beasts except that early on I gave up any plans of becoming a millionaire through the art of medicine.

As for experiments of the undangerous and un-totally gross kind, I've had moderate success with such things as letting the air out of a balloon and watching it fly frantically around the room or getting tarnish off a penny with baking soda.

Just don't ask me to explain what it all means. I mean, if I could explain it, I could be on *Nova* myself, right? And everybody knows that only experts are on *Nova*. So not being an expert only makes sense. Somebody's got to be in the audience, for heaven's sake. If everybody were an expert, why even bother to have shows like *Nova?*

The Pennsylvania Department of Education disagrees. Figures. They're the same sinister league that forces ignorant children into science fairs.

Part 4

∞

Just Between You and Me
and the Crayon on the Walls

∞

Fighting the Pack-Rat Gene —
One Mound at a Time

For next Mother's Day, I want something you can't put a price on: nothing. It's the only thing I have room for.

When we bought our home, my husband and I knew we had to get something big to house our growing family. We purchased a city row with five bedrooms on a double lot. Set atop a steep hill, the place looked huge. Our oldest child was then twenty-four inches tall, while her baby sister measured about a foot in circumference. After ten years and three more kids, the walls of our house are closing in on people and debris like the trash compactor in *Star Wars*.

Over the years, I have made regular trips to community drop-off bins and sold my valuables to strangers for a dime at yard sales, all to no avail. I still haven't been able to dig out. My husband is a saver.

It is a well-known fact that the pack-rat gene skips a generation. My mom had it to the point that dusting became a trip down memory lane. She saved bits of crayon, old seed catalogs, and items that could be exhibited on the *Antiques Roadshow*. But even that was manageable until she started adopting other people's stuff. Once, during the hippie decade, when churches were divesting themselves of statues, she brought home an eight-foot figure of St. Paul clutching a sword and deposited it in our basement. The statue wore long flowing gray hair and beard and a wild look. The meter man had to be resuscitated. My husband's mother, on the other hand, puts out the kind of trash that people like my mom slow down for.

So far, our kids are gross materialists. Their favorite saying is, "Don't throw that out! I was planning to play with it someday!"

For a while I tried deception. "Mom, what happened to that big pink loofa lamp thingy that fizzes when you talk to it?" "I don't know," I answered with a shrug. It wasn't a lie. The garbage truck had taken it six months before, and after that I lost track of it.

This system was actually working pretty well until one night, after hauling three-quarters of the contents of the basement out to the curb while my husband was at work, I caught him hauling half of it onto the front porch. Apparently he wanted to fight in front of the neighbors. "This is a good, solid chair!" he declared. I tried to argue that the only solid part about it was thirteen coats of paint. But when he enfolded a pair of broken training wheels in a fond embrace, bit his lower lip, and accused, "How could you get rid of these? They belonged to our children!" — I knew I had to change my tactics. "Well now how did those get out there?" I said, shaking my head in feigned surprise. It would have to wait until his next business trip.

It's an uphill battle; and I'm not sure I want to know what's at the top of the heap.

For moral support I consulted the experts: a decorating magazine with such promising articles as "Create More Living Space" and "Clutter-Free Kids' Rooms." But I didn't get past the first photo: a coffee table displaying a large glass vase, under which rested a stack of newly minted picture books. Behind it sat two grinning boys. Their feet wore clean white socks and dangled off the edge of a pale yellow divan.

No wonder the boys looked like they were having fun. They had obviously been dropped onto the sofa by helicopter just before the photographer shot them.

I threw the magazine in the garbage, camouflaging it under eggshells, coffee grounds, and used paper plates, just in case my husband was nearby.

It's every mother's dilemma: how to create a home that is clean and comfortable, knowing exactly how much materialism will do the trick.

A bigger house might be the answer. But I doubt it. Bigger houses have been statistically proven to cause bigger clutter. And I can't blame my husband completely. Much as I fight it, somewhere in my genetic make-up, a recessive curbside-shopping gene got in. I first noticed it back in the days when we were newly married students trying to beat the high cost of living in the Austrian Alps. Many items that others had discarded formed the backdrop of some of our happiest years. Amidst such simplicity our firstborn arrived.

Lots of people would say the answer is fewer kids. But as much as the thought of empty space appeals to me, I could never wish it to be that empty. Besides, Pope John Paul says that siblings, not possessions, build character.

Hey, maybe that's it! If children build character, ours surely won't mind if I just get rid of a few extra bags of their toys. If the Pope says they don't need them, that's good enough for me.

∞

Family Prayer: An Occasion of Sin

Catholics and the Rosary. You can sing it to the tune of "Love and Marriage." Well, not exactly. It's a little off-beat. Then again, so are a lot of Rosaries.

Every night, when we were kids and had just finished up the supper dishes, my Mom would say, "You know what would be a good thing to do right now?" She always said it in the same tone, as if it had never occurred to her before.

We'd grit our teeth and grumble, "Say the Rosary." Then we'd drag ourselves into the living room, flop to our knees, and bury our faces in the sofa.

Compared with now, those days were the pinnacle of my spiritual growth.

My husband subscribes to the theory of the Teachable Moment. It's where you take a routine activity, break it down into Thomistic bites, explain them, contradict them, contradict the contradictions, then give a quiz. He's one of those husbands homeschooling mothers dream about. Thoroughly convinced, totally into it, dying to be made a part of it.

Much as I appreciate the enthusiasm, at the end of the day the last thing I want is a teachable moment. My days are full of them.

Please Don't Drink the Holy Water!

They haunt my confessions. "Sin of omission number twelve this week, Father: another teachable moment lost."

By bedtime, the only thing I want to teach the children is how to stand still while I position the catapult.

Yet, inevitably, we still haven't said the Rosary. This is the worst teachable moment of them all.

With a sigh, I kneel down and begin reciting it the way I was taught at my mother's knee: the *rosarius rapidus*.

The *rosarius rapidus* was good enough for us — sleek, high performance, goes from 0 to 60 in 5.4 Hail Marys, with plenty of extras.

Greg is writing a tract to show why that version is invalid. According to him, there is only One True Rosary. It must contain the following attributes:

Atmosphere
We begin with a moment of silence. This is to get everyone calm and collected and in a meditative mood. With five girls, this takes half an hour.

In contrast, the *rosarius rapidus* begins by starting without everybody. As soon as I fire off the Sign of the Cross, they come crashing to their knees like privates in front of a drill sergeant. Instant piety.

During Greg's imposition of silence, there are protests, interruptions, whispers, hands raised, groans, sign language, and threats.

After threats, it's time for:

Intentions
Miss Firstborn makes a preemptive strike. "For everybody!"

Nice try, kid. Really a chip off the old block. I shake my head knowingly. So much to learn.

Her dad deafly proceeds, "For Janet, a lady who called me at work. She's the daughter of Mrs. Coalbean from Iowa, an old friend of ours from the Contra Episcopate days. She moved out there to be near her mother because she's an invalid. . . . "

Miss Number Four breaks in, "Daddy, what's an invalid?"

"Look it up in the dictionary!" somebody snaps from behind.

Miss Firstborn gets blamed and protests innocence. She is corrected for talking back. Out of a sense of honor, I step forward and admit the infraction. I receive the first meaningful glare.

My penance continues, "Invalids, honey, are persons who are sick; sometimes they can't get out of bed. They need others to help them."

"Like Ruth?"

"That's right, sweetie, like Ruth, yes."

"Can we get on with it?"

I receive the second meaningful glare.

"For your information, Janet may be dying!"

"Me, too!" groans Miss Firstborn. Titters trickle up from the other children.

Greg's face automatically slackens into a well-worn, "They're all against me 'cuz I'm the only guy," expression.

Miss Four helps to smooth things over by continuing with the intentions. "For Uncle Ted, that he finds someone to buy his business speedibably and profibably."

A broad grin spreads over Dad's face. She said it just the way he has been saying it for the past two years. He pauses to rumple her hair.

The Creed gets underway and goes smoothly enough, thanks to a crack fourth-century editorial team. A passing nod at faith, hope, and charity and we're off.

From now on, it's touch and go.

Please Don't Drink the Holy Water!

The Quiz Game

"The First Glorious Mystery," my husband intones. I hold my breath while he continues. "Anyone? Anyone?" Hands shoot up from the younger children. Miss Teen groans.

"The Announcement!" shouts Number Four.

"No. . . . " says her dad.

"The Visitating? The Presentating?"

"No — we're in the Glorious, sweetheart." He starts giving hints, "the Re —, the Re —"

"The Rejoicing?"

"The Res —, the Resu —"

"The Resurrection!"

"Very good, Mommy. Why'd you have to do that? She almost got it." He delivers the third meaningful glare.

By now, any illusions I may have had about getting into a meditative mood have been shattered. This is my own fault, since I was fool enough to pray for patience one time. I decide to look motherly and get the baby out of the playpen.

Besides with three meaningful glares already, I need to deflect blame to an alternate scapegoat.

The Entertainment

The toddler (current or otherwise) is a natural exhibitionist. She can sense a captive audience. We're short, immobile, and most conveniently pointed in the same direction.

The toddler takes a minute to warm up while we proceed with the meditation before the first decade. "The holy women went with the first dawn to the tomb, and what did they find there? Anyone?"

The *Aves* begin, and she's off. The first event is toddling adorably from one person to another until everyone has been informed, via a hug or a shove, depending on the mood, that the baby is about to perform.

A gymnastic exhibition ensues.

Every piece of furniture is climbed upon. Toddler relaxes in it for two seconds, dangles a pair of naked feet, and giggles. All eyes are now on her, except her dad's, which are closed. The climax of the opening act takes place on a moving stage: the swivel rocker. She whirls around, peeking over the top and around the sides, grinning, blinking, and squealing.

Then comes the main event: an exhibition of strength, will, and agility that would make a greased pig jealous. Toddler grabs the step stool, Miss Firstborn and I dive for it, colliding in midair as she fakes and dodges under us. She escapes without a dent just in the nick of time. She begins running around the room with the stool legs pointing dangerously out toward people, furniture, and — most chillingly of all — drywall. It crashes into its place beside the piano. The baby mounts it like an elephant, and begins hammering on the keys.

The entire audience has turned to face the piano — except Dad. The Rosary continues in the background because a) Dad hasn't noticed the racket, and b) no one wants to risk making him notice it.

Dancing concludes the entertainment. This is the *pièce de résistance*. No amount of threatening, "Don't look at her," can wrest their feminine eyes from her. She senses she is appreciated and begins singing.

The children collapse into fits of admiration. They begin jostling to be the first one to leap upon her and smother her with kisses. This brings the curtain down on the show, as she falls under the heap and issues helpless muffled cries. A scuffle gets underway as each one attempts to extract a limb until . . .

Dad notices.

The Sermon

∞

Fight Reruns

Ever wonder what married couples fight about? It's not the kind of question you can just go up and ask people, but human-interest polls list money, how to raise the kids, jobs, which channel to watch, and in-laws. While this may be factual in the particulars, I maintain that all real fights are about one thing: love.

We had been married several years before it dawned on me that all of our fights are reruns. In fact, no matter how they get started, there is really only one basic fight theme. They're kind of like Shakespeare's comedies or Dickens's novels: there's only one formula. In Shakespeare you have cross-dressing, long-lost relatives in disguise, and a marriage at the end. Dickens serves up unblemished virgins and boys toiling in sweat shops. In our marital squabbles, the dialogue never changes. It always boils down to:

Me: You just don't care!
Him: I don't understand. . . .

Women want to know that their husbands care. Greg says that is the kind of thinking that got Bill Clinton elected twice. It isn't logical, it isn't rational, and nothing can induce him to understand it.

What Greg fails to understand about me is what I've been telling him for years. *He doesn't have to figure me out.*

To be fair, it wasn't always this way. During our first few years of married life, I thought that when I was miserable, it should be obvious to him. I sat around sending snitty vibes that just bounced back at me and made me even snittier.

It was going nowhere. I'd end up lying awake mad while he snored comfortably beside me, oblivious to the pain and suffering he had caused.

His attitude has always been that I should just tell him straight whatever is on my mind. But I've been doing that for several years now and not having much better results. Whatever I tell him seems to come out in translation about as near the real thing as a Mormon bible.

Take, for example, a typical quarrel that ends in my telling Greg to go away. What do you think he does next? He goes away.

He just doesn't get it.

Every woman knows that "Go away" means stay and keep trying to make up.

Afterward he falls immediately asleep, and I lie awake trying to convince myself I don't care. For years I have envied his serotonin gland to the point of bloodlust. Somewhere in his enviable ancestry is the person who coined the phrase, "Well, this certainly is bad news, but I wouldn't lose any sleep over it." Whereas back in my ancestry is the person who invented the alarm clock and then lay awake wondering if he set it correctly. Finally I can hold out no longer. I wake him up. Then he has the gall to act genuinely surprised to see me and annoyed that I am waking him up.

Finally, with a little forceful persuasion, he computes that the problem is that when I told him to go away, he failed to stick around and patch things up. This is further evidence that he didn't care.

This was fine for the first ten years we were married, but I am not getting any younger.

So lately, I have taken to writing things down, which I think is pretty accommodating of me. Men need to see things in writing. Who do you think invented crib notes?

But hey, it's okay. I'm an open book.

Just so there would be no more confusion I wrote:

The psyche of woman is such that "Go away" is said when the man has either a) been away too long, or b) done something wrong. The worst thing he can do at this point is go away. He should stay and attempt to show he cares. Moreover, he must keep this up until she is convinced he cares, or she will irreparably hate him.

I put the note in a little book in the nightstand, right on the back of a note I got from him a few years ago pledging not to criticize any more new haircuts.

This was to stress its importance. The haircut note is a very important document that I'd keep in a safe deposit box if it were convenient. It keeps us from having a two-hour argument that ends:

Him: What are you mad at me for? Your hairdresser's the one who's crippled!

Me: You could shut me up with two little words.

Him: What?

Me: I'm sorry I criticized your haircut. I was wrong. You look fabulous!

The note also saves energy for the real fights that end in: "Go away."

The next time I told him to go away and he did, I lay awake giving him ample time to reference the rule on the back of the haircut note. After about two hours, I woke him up and showed it to him. He opened one eye in a gesture of diplomatic toleration and said, "I don't care what you do with your hair. It's three o'clock in the morning."

Me: You just don't care!
Him: I don't understand. . . .

He had forgotten all about the rule. Maybe we just don't fight enough.

∞

The Extracurricular Activity for Dummies

"Hello. My name is Susie, and I'm an extracurricular activity-aholic."

You know how these things get started: you just want to experiment a little, see what all the hype is about. Oh, you play it safe at first — get the oldest kid piano lessons, in the privacy and security of your home. You tell yourself she can quit anytime. . . .

Before the first year is out, you've put a hundred thousand miles on the minivan running your kids to horseback riding, ice dancing, karate, classical acting, snow sculpting, and Lego Club.

And do the kids want this? Don't ask me. I don't know. I'm too busy living vicariously to ask them.

My mom never let me join things. I was the last of eight, which meant that her activities gene had gotten worn out way before I was born.

I am different. As a parent, I believe in listening to my kids. I care about their needs. I'm in tune with their aspirations. If they want something and it is something that I always wanted but my mother wouldn't let me have, they get it.

There was one thing that our kids really wanted, though, that I dreaded.

Please Don't Drink the Holy Water!

A puppy.

Now, I happen to love dogs. I really do. We had two when I was a child. We also had a garage, a game room with a hard floor, an acre or so of property, and no leash laws.

Our first dog, Lobo, a virile lab/husky mix, roamed all day and came home for supper, usually covered with whatever was dead and stinking in the woods across the street. To add to the fun, we had farmland about forty miles outside of town. Lobo loved nothing better than to peel out of the car, frolic all day in swamp, carcass, and burr, and return exhausted when we called him back at quitting time. One day he returned sooner than usual — about two minutes, to be precise. He had found a critter than could bite back. There were dozens, possibly hundreds of quills in his muzzle, ears, face, and throat. We put his trembling heap back into the station wagon, turned it around, and forgot about harvesting potatoes that day. From that day on, whenever we got within smelling distance of his vet, that big virile dog reverted to that same trembling heap. He blamed it all on the vet. As far as the porcupine was concerned, he never knew what hit him. This was obvious because a few weeks after he recovered, it hit him again.

In spite of the constant baths, the vet visits, the afternoons spent picking hundreds of burrs out of his long hair, we loved that dog. He loved us, too. He couldn't stand to see us leave. Since he was never tied up, this meant he was hard to shake. His favorite domestic pastime was chasing cars. He gave every car that came by a good go, but he regarded our car as his special turf. On a couple of occasions, he chased us all the way into town, and we worried he'd get himself lost or killed. So every time we went somewhere, we had to drive around the neighborhood to wear him out. When he finally flopped down in somebody's yard, panting with his feet up in the air, it was safe to leave.

The Extracurricular Activity for Dummies

Perhaps it was because of my dog experiences as a child that I held out for so long against my own kids. I found myself talking like my mother. "We'll see. . . . Maybe when you're older. . . . You can't just start this you know; you'd have to finish it. . . . Do you know how much work is involved?"

I mean, there are boundaries. And let's face it: some things your kids ask for tend to sneak beyond them to poop.

Our second dog, Grigio, a black lab, was a sneak about his excretions. He was a fundamentally good boy. He hated to disappoint us. So when he was cooped up too long, he would place his duty in a dark corner and hope it would go unnoticed. Unfortunately, one day he landed it on a model house my father was building. It was to be a reconstruction of the farmhouse he grew up in, which had recently been destroyed by fire. Using old photos, he had taken great care over the details and scale. My mother showed it to me in horror one day, yellow and dripping. There was nothing to do but plunge it into the nearest trash can. Luckily my father had left off working on it, and it was weeks before he looked for it again. My mom defied her strict *Baltimore Catechism* upbringing and pretended ignorance. She and I made a believable show of looking for it, too. We loved Grigio too much to turn him in.

Yes, I had loved our dogs. Unconditionally loved them — which is the kind of love dogs demand. Even love, however, cannot erase the memory of the sheer amount of work and mess involved.

Still, the kids kept it up. They couldn't understand why I was so reluctant. Just because we have a city row home with a city-size yard, with no garage and way too much carpeting, was no reason to be so stingy.

I began to soften. After all, all they wanted was a simple pet. Was that so much to ask? Something to bark and refuse to fetch and open up a whole new dimension of their personalities.

Please Don't Drink the Holy Water!

I began surreptitiously looking at dog books in the library. Maybe there was some breed out there with minimal shedding and excreting qualities. . . .

Then I saw it. A book from Target Publications. It was about a little girl who had raised the softest little lab pup named Lovey. After a year, the girl heroically gave Lovey up to an organization that trained him for a boy who needed him. By the last page, I was in tears.

How could I have been so blind? Right before my eyes, a *teachable moment!*

Not only a pet, but also the chance to do something for the greater community. The benefits of sacrificing for someone else would be immeasurable. The kids would grow as individuals, learn responsibility, become civic-minded. Best of all, temporary dog ownership!

I ran home, looked up the local Target Office, and talked my husband into attending a meeting.

When we entered that puppy-filled room, our kids went into a cuteness swoon.

We signed on the dotted line.

Perhaps I should record the experience in a diary, I thought. Someday I could present each of my children a bound copy — perhaps on her wedding day.

9-28-99: Target is only twenty miles up the road! We went to one of the meetings. It looks ideal. We'd get the dog for about a year; after which he would enter the training program, graduate in harness, and make us proud. Maybe I could call it my science curriculum this year — or even gym. Greg wants a male lab so that he will have an ally in the house. They're unbeatable with kids.

I can still see Lobo: the cute way his ears would stand up when a pompom hat came into view. A brown streak, going at a thirty-mile-per-hour clip, a flash of teeth, a screaming but perfectly safe child. So gentle.

9-30-99: My friend Leslie doesn't approve. She thinks it's mean to get a dog for your kids and then send him off after a year. I reminded her that at least when he's no longer with us, we'll know he's still alive.

Besides, I had always wanted to be in Target when I was a kid, and my mother wouldn't let me.

11-18-99: Klupper arrived today! He is a warm, fluffy, seven-week-old shiny black bundle of Labrador-love!

The only problem I foresee is that the kids give him no peace. I'm going to have to teach them to leave him alone. When they finally got done mauling him, he peed on the floor. A cute little puddle. Poor guy.

Wow! The Target leader told me that Klupper cost the organization $25,000! I hope we don't teach him bad habits or lose him or let him get run over. The guy was reassuring, though. He gave me a waiver to sign where we mutually agreed not to sue each other.

And if there is ever a problem, we just contact Muddy-paws. That's the local club. They are there to help. All we have to do is attend monthly meetings, demos, training seminars, public-service events, and dog-biscuit bake sales. Sounds like fun! This is just the thing to keep the kids busy so I can have some down time.

1-10-00: I've finally gotten through the puppy-raising man-ual that the Target guy dropped off. A small mountain of literature to match the growing mountain of dog. I read it cover to cover to make sure we are doing everything right. Here are some of the rules:

Rule 1: Aggression

It is very important to your puppy's future life as a working dog that we begin proper training right from the beginning.

Your puppy must learn to obey you out of love, not fear. You must never, ever hit him. Most of all, you are to curb any latent aggressive tendencies. You will need one choke chain and one cage that could sleep a lion.

Greg is definitely working against me in this one. The introduction of the first other male in the household has done something to him. The two have bonded. Klupper thinks Greg is Jesse Ventura. We are tracking his growth by the size and height of the tears on Greg's pants. I'm worried. They say that once this breed has tasted cotton, it's too late.

Rule 2: Potty training

Your puppy must do his business on command. He mustn't mark territory in the neighborhood, but must go like a gentleman at home. How would it be for his future owner to stop at every telephone pole? The procedure is really quite simple. Position yourself beside your puppy, praising his efforts and making sure he does not lift his leg.

The guy takes a half-hour. We're managing by a schedule taped to the refrigerator door. Each of us takes turns standing by him, and cheering him on in front of the entire neighborhood. I think it stresses him out. After he comes in, he relaxes and goes on the floor. We then mark his chart with a 1 or a 2.

Rule 3: Castration, although necessary, is not allowed

We're sorry, but in case your puppy turns out to be suitable for breeding, we cannot curb his aggression with castration. We realize that this is illogical because we never use aggressive dogs for breeding anyway.

Klupper's first crime was to claim the TV set as his own. Like any guilty child, he gave it away by trying to slink past me without looking me in the eye. My response was a spontaneous karate demonstration which impressed my children as much as Klupper. "Anyone who tells the club about this will get the same," I growled. Klupper understood.

Rule 4: Feeding

Your puppy must not develop a taste for anything but expensive regulation expensive dog expensive food. Absolutely no table scraps! How would it be if someday he were to whine and salivate in a restaurant?

Deprived of the usual doggie delicacies, Klupper has developed a taste for rabbit raisins. He likes them, but they don't like him. Muddypaws suggested Pepto, but he turns his nose up at it.

Rule Summary

Your puppy must never, never act like a dog.

4-1-00: I'm expecting.

6-2-00: Second day in a row, have failed to make bed. Klupper is sick. Haven't gotten dressed either — not such a problem since slept in clothes. Husband is robust as ever. Has been getting to work early lately. Has a reason to: Klupper. He is so sick, it is sickening. Has been eating rabbit raisins again. Only have a few more months to curb him of this before Target recalls him. Feel I have gambled $25,000 of someone else's money and lost it.

6-3-00: Klupper and I recovering. Gave him a bath. Gave self a bath. Did hair first time since Sunday. Look under forty again.

7-11-00: Klupper has become a local celebrity now that he's the size of a donkey.

He has reached the troubled period of a parent's life called adolescence. According to Muddypaws, many find the transition to adolescence difficult. True. I find myself using his cage more and more. He can't get me in there.

Rule 5 in the puppy manual states: Your puppy must be walked every day, rain or shine, snow, sleet, or gloom. He must not be allowed to tug on the leash, lag behind, or sniff things.

I've taken to paying the kids for each go-around. Klupper's size and urges are reminiscent of Henry VIII's. By contrast, the girls are stubbornly maintaining their present stature, and I am growing progressively fatter and weaker. But so far, we are still in the game. I like to think this is inspiring cooperation amongst the girls. It takes three of them to manage him.

It seems the whole neighborhood is taking an interest. The girls inform me that every evening, when the neighbors discover they are walking Klupper, the blue TV lights in their windows go out. Apparently the local entertainment we're providing is better. A few of the polite neighbors pull back their curtains. The others come out on their porches, spray themselves with Bug-off, and open a beer.

Child One, on the left, holds a leash attached to a choke chain. Child Two, on the right, holds a second leash attached to what some salesman named a "tamer." This is a cousin of the muzzle and is supposed to drive a dog into submission. Following One and Two is Child Three — the designated runner. Child Three's job is to run home screaming, "Mom, he got away again!" I then go around the neighborhood rattling a box of biscuits. Greg's job is to remain at work in an air-conditioned office that does not have dog poop on the carpet, come home late, and claim to be too exhausted to help out.

Baths are another big draw. I am thinking of selling tickets. Neighbors line up along our fence. They hoist the shorter children into our tree. The puppy manual doesn't give a set procedure for baths. They just expect you to take care of it as needed. For a dog whose fragrance of choice is Eau de Diarrhée , baths get pretty regular. The kids have hit on a good system. They get into bathing suits. Then they get Klupper rigged as if for a walk. Child One then sits on him, Child Two lathers, and Child Three dangles a biscuit just out of reach. Child Four hands out programs.

11-9-00: Target came to pick up Klupper today. The kids miss him, but should get over it once the baby comes. If Klupper doesn't pass, they're going to offer him back to us — to keep. Help!

12-15-00: Little Bernadette was born today. Everyone is thrilled. My husband says I asked the doctor what I'd had, "human or canine." Must have been the drugs.

Looking forward to getting some rest. . . .

∞

Never Let 'Em See You Rest

How is it that kids have radar for when you're not up to speed? It must be something in the atmospheric pressure that makes their energy levels go up when Mom's goes down.

I am not talking about being actually sick. What I'm talking about here is that phenomenon called "just tired." It's the middle ground between health and sickness. You feel done in, worn out, uptight, and downtrodden, but you're still on your feet. This signals to everyone that you are open for business. Traffic continues to pour into your mental office.

"Mom, the baby drank the holy water again!"

"Mom, she threw glue in my hair when I didn't throw glue in hers!"

Your nerves put in for a transfer to a Trappist monastery. Soon the only sudden noises you can tolerate are coming from you.

Sickness, on the other hand, is like going on vacation. When I am sick, there are no sweeter nurses than my five daughters. It's a rare occasion that catches me staggering around before lowering myself gingerly onto the couch, and they never fail to respond with heartwarming sympathy. They rush to my side saying, "Aww...." All sibling combatants call an immediate cease-fire. A shared maternal gene activates, and I am massaged, waited on, and com-forted beyond anything my mom ever did. In fact, I prefer them to my mom. Her version of a cure-all was an enema.

None of the above applies, however, if I happen to be "just tired." While "sick" runs smoothly, "just tired" still has a lot of kinks in it.

In order to gather sympathy and cooperation from the girls, "just tired" has to go through an overload. Overloads are not pretty. Overloads involve shouting, turning alternating shades of red and white, then involuntary tears and collapse. You then get the benefit of the sick treatment because, of course, by then you are sick. I am not sure it's worth it.

Of course, one may always try hiding. Mothers with big houses or an outbuilding such as a detached garage, toolshed, or tree house may succeed in this. It is very difficult if you have a row home containing five ever-present homeschooled children. Still, it's easier than overload. I wait for a time when they are engrossed in something like schoolwork or quiet play or a girl fight, and I dis-appear, say, to my room. Immediately their sensors activate, and they leave off writhing on the floor en masse and release the arti-cle that was moments before precious enough to maim and be maimed for and begin roaming the house saying, "Where's Mom?" A thorough search of our house takes fifteen seconds. They begin with the bathroom and search everywhere except certain areas of the basement we call the dungeon — where they know I also dare not go. Finally, they knock on my door, sometimes all at once (explosion style), sometimes in a steady trickle (Chinese water-torture style).

That, too, isn't worth it. The other alternative is to rest right out in the open. I lay my weary frame down on the couch with a cup of soothing herbal tea steaming nearby. Two p.m. Good. A whole hour before the neighbors get home from school and launch the doorbell. I hope the kids will see me and commence tiptoeing and keeping their voices down.

"Oh, poor Mommy. She's all alone in the dark."

The phone rings. Thirty pairs of feet gallop to answer it. "Hello?" A fight breaks out.

"That's not fair. I was going for it, and she grabbed it! Mom!"

"You always get it. Besides, I was there first."

"No fair! I called it before you even got up."

I'm wondering who could be on the other end listening to this, but I'm too tired to be embarrassed. It turns out to be my husband. He asks me to pray for Mrs. Coalbean's daughter Janet. Her kids are acting up, and she has had a terrible bout with insomnia because of it. I let him know that I'm trying to grab a nap. He apologizes and asks why the heck I don't unplug the phone. Good point. After we hang up, I do just that.

Now there won't be any more disruptions. I concentrate on drifting.

Through the haze I detect a steady pounding. An airplane flying overhead perhaps. . . . No, it's three pairs of feet, tangled with chairs on a ceramic tile floor. The only child-approved method of getting up from a chair entails a shoving motion with the arms so that both chair and table both travel at equal speeds away from one another, leaving enough room for child to spring lithely to her feet. The approved method of sitting down entails child dragging the chair over the tile while simultaneously hurling herself into it — creating a safe crash landing every time.

Soon a foreign sound is introduced. Am I dreaming, or is it . . . an ankle jump rope. One of the children is discovering how many jumps it will take to go twenty feet on the tile floor. Even in my condition, this is easy to decipher, because she counts the jumps aloud, making sure she can hear herself over the ten-pound weight on the end. Background noise ceases and the ankle jump rope is the only sound. The other three kids have noticed the game. I know what I will hear next:

"My turn!"

"No, I was next!"

"Let go! I just got it!

"Quit hogging it!"

. . . followed by a stampede to where the first jump-rope child started. All four arrive at the spot at the same time. A succession of sickening thuds signals a collision. Then each one begins trying to beat the first one's count.

This is out of hand. I rouse myself just enough to shout at them to stop. In a show of prompt obedience, the three children who do not have possession of the ankle jump rope pile themselves upon the one who does and compete to wrench it off her foot. The wearer shrieks. The others shout her down: "Mom said knock off the noise!" The child cries that it isn't fair. She didn't get two chances when everyone else did. She appeals to me. I scream, "Let her have a turn!"

This is not sane behavior.

Warning circuits are on. This is the last stop before overload. I leap off the couch and warn the kids to get out of range. Each child tries to whine an octave higher than the rest. The current youngest, Destructo Tot, wakes up from a fifteen-minute nap that was supposed to last an hour. I proclaim that by evening I expect to receive a cumulative total of four hundred sentences on disturbing the peace.

Ten minutes later, the kids are writing away, Tot is off somewhere, probably writing on the wall, and there is a lull in the noise.

I try again. All I need is twenty minutes. Just twenty measly minutes to snuggle up under a blanket with my now-tepid tea and read *Purgatory: A Second There Is Worth Ten Lifetimes in a Concentration Camp*, and drop cozily off to sleep. I've even taken a mild sedative to help me along.

Please Don't Drink the Holy Water!

I begin drifting . . . unconscious of the passing of time. I'm between two worlds, partially aware by a crick in my neck that I'm propped up on the couch, yet steadily entering into the beginnings of a dream, when a child approaches with a question. She leans down in my face and whispers, "What were we supposed to write a hundred times?"

Another child shouts from the kitchen, "I will not disturb the peace of the household, *duh*!"

"In cursive or regular?" she shouts back.

"Who cares? She never reads it anyway," comes the answer.

"In pen or pencil?"

I handle this one: "Blood."

Child gets the message and leaves. I concentrate on drifting. A second child enters. Since I'm so tired, she has a good idea that will save us all a lot of work. "Remember that package of M&Ms that melted and you said to put it in the freezer? Well, could I get it out, and could we eat it, and could we maybe write this down as a science experiment and be done with science for the day?" The remaining two children hear her and come in to tell me that they are sorry they were bad and bothered me today. The first child returns, pronounces, "Sshhh!!!" like a boiling kettle and yells at the others to be quiet, and can't they see that Mom is resting? I tell them to go and eat the candy.

They chase each other into the kitchen.

A struggle ensues. Shattering glass is heard, then finally, silence. The kind of silence that comes right after a tornado.

Eight more hours. Only eight more hours to wait until I can go to bed.

I get up off the couch and go see what's the matter.

A simple broken glass. But trying to get to the bottom of such an incident is like facing the O.J. defense team. It's a rotten thing to say about your own flesh and blood, but my children are born lawyers.

Team Spokesperson: Sorry, Mom, it was an accident!

Me (sounding like my mother): Accidents are when you're washing a glass and it slips from your hand. Waste is when the two of you have the stupidity to fight when one of you has a glass in her hand.

T.S.: We weren't fighting. We were struggling.

Me: Whatever. Struggling with a glass in your hand.

T.S.: The glass wasn't in anyone's hand. It was on the counter.

Me: Okay. Struggling with a glass on the counter when you should have known that your flailing elbows could knock it over.

T.S.: I didn't knock it over with my elbow. I was reaching up to slap her face, and I moved my elbow, and it knocked off.

Second Member of Team: That's true, Mom. I saw it!

Justice has been served. They were fighting and are now on the same side against me.

Now, my husband and I are fortunate to have honest children, children who know their catechism, children who go to weekly confession.

They do not lie. They shift the blame.

"It wasn't me. It was the inanimate object's fault. *It* got in the way of the path of my elbow, *it* knocked off, *it* fell on the floor, and that is why *it* is getting exactly what it deserves by being broken into a million pieces. Why make such a fuss about it, Mom? Don't you think *it* has been punished enough?"

Having kids has made me a believer. I no longer think the excuses you see on judge shows are staged. When Queenticia Jackson was charged with assault, she vehemently denied throwing a chair at Keira Sloane. "I did not throw that chair at her. I most certainly did not! It hit her over the head!" Well, now, that's another story.

Or the one about the accident reports. A man filed a deposition that went something like: "The telephone pole was approaching fast. I swerved to avoid it, but it just kept on coming. Finally, it hit me." I used to think that was made up, but no more. That is just the sort of logic kids give you.

All I wanted to do was take a twenty-minute power nap so that I could return to educating the children in faith and culture, so as to bequeath to them the tools necessary to know, love, and serve God and be happy in this world and in the next.

There's no chance of that now. It's three p.m., and the doorbell's ringing. . . .

∞

Lent Is Coming.
Will Your Looks Survive?

Educational experts often express worry about homeschooling cooping up the kids, but who ever considers the parents? I, for one, have been known to howl at the moon during Lent.

Lent is the homeschooler's longest mile. The kids get their daily constitutional bouncing off the walls, the clutter has built up so long that it has evolved the power of reproduction, and I tell myself I'm not really behind on this year's work: I'm ahead of last year's.

Once you've passed Christmas, psychologically you feel half-way done with your 180-day school year. On paper, however, you could have as many as 105 more days. This at a time when darkness descends before supper, when the jagged brown branches of naked trees scratch the grey dome of a mournful sky, and islands of mud and straw-like grass appear amid random piles of black snow. The multicolored Christmas lights have long come down. There are no diverting holiday parties; there's no windfall of presents to look forward to; and all the bills have come due.

The Real World tries to make up for the general malaise by hawking Valentine's Day as soon as New Year's is over. Candy, flowers, diamonds, dinner at an expensive restaurant — glamor plus *amour*. And who are they selling it to? Men, presumably. But who really cares about this stuff? Women.

I have never met a woman yet who does not take Valentine's Day seriously. Meanwhile, men, who are still recovering from the Christmas bills, have no idea why every Valentine's Day ends up like this:

"Honey, why are you crying?"

"Because you don't care!"

"What? I brought home flowers."

"It's the least you can do. If you really loved me, you'd have gotten the Sweetheart Floral Arrangement with Diamond Bracelet for an Additional $300, that says, 'For all the things you do, there's no better way to say: I love you.' The commercials have been on for a month. You just don't love me!"

A month later comes St. Patrick's Day. Most men appreciate this holiday mainly because the female public has not yet learned to expect presents. (It also offers a great excuse for interrupting Lent with a drunken orgy — just as the saint would have wanted.)

In our house, we also have a devotion to good St. Joseph, whose feast comes two days after St. Patrick's. We've taken up the Italian custom of celebrating it as Father's Day, dutifully observing it as a holiday from school and Lent.

After that, it's back to penance.

Around this time, I start fantasizing about sending the kids to school. Idyllic images from my youth bubble to the surface of my consciousness: the kids trudging through the slush in the frigid pre-dawn. My right hand presses a warm coffee mug to my bosom while the other waves goodbye in slow motion from behind the window.

There is only one remedy for this: television.

TV is a great way to motivate the girls to get their work done. "Finish your math, pick up your stuff, clear the table, wash your face, eat your beans, put away your school books. . . . " Not just one activity, but all of them can be done if there is a movie at the end.

Now, I know that people are wondering what is wrong with my spiritual life. Why didn't I say that prayer is the remedy, instead of television?

Keep in mind we are in Lent here. Fasting, abstinence, and extra devotions are all great stuff. They help us to purge our imaginations of the low things of earth and elevate them to the thought of heaven. But we still need something to get the kids to sit still and be quiet.

So our family gives up everything but holy movies. A compromise, but it's better than murder.

Dramas about the saints are entertaining and uplifting, and you never have to worry about bad scenes or bad language. At least, that's what I used to think.

One day I put on a film about St. Vincent de Paul and then left the room in peaceful assurance. Halfway through the movie, I checked in to find the girls huddled together behind the couch, casting lots to determine who would be the brave one and shut it off. It was an old foreign film, and brutally unsentimental. When I walked in, the dying poor were grabbing the beds out from under their cold companions. They weren't the deserving, sweet poor with whom you could sympathize. They were hostile, ugly, and criminal. I personally loved the film. It showed St. Vincent's job as it probably really was. As far as the kids were concerned, though, it would take a couple of cartoons to purge it from their imaginations.

Please Don't Drink the Holy Water!

What with the dreary weather, the cabin fever, and the emphasis decidedly away from personal vanity, Lent is also the time when we are most vulnerable to the ill effects of Frump.

Frump. It's like those slippery-slope things the catechism warns you about. If you allow yourself to get complacent about venial frump, before you know it you find yourself inordinately attached to it. Before you know it, you are immersed in a lifestyle of mortal frump. You are a frumpaholic!

I never thought it could happen to me. For several years, I had been holding steady at age twenty-three. I was young. Young and with it. I even took having kids in stride. I was permed and fit and energetic enough to paint my bedroom while seven months into my third pregnancy. Then it happened. I woke up one morning, looked in the mirror, and somebody's mother looked back.

I trace it back to the evening I put a little black waddle skirt on a hanger. The next morning it had gained eight inches, an elastic waist, and turned denim. I whirled around and demanded an explanation from my husband. He claimed he had nothing to do with it and even had the temerity to blame it on thrift-store dependency.

Desperately I began rifling through the closet. It was a blue sea of denim. Some of the jumpers and skirts had a well-worn look at the knees, like they'd suffered under too many Rosaries.

I had no choice but to put one on. The rest is a blur. I faintly remember something bulging in one of the pockets. It was purple. I always did look good in purple. I pinned it to my sweater, borrowed my husband's best warm, wooly socks, and slipped on a pair of flats. I put my hair in a ponytail, looked in the mirror, and said aloud, "I sure hope the doorbell doesn't ring today."

When my husband got home that night, he asked why I was wearing a grape lollipop and why the toddler wouldn't let me out of her sight.

Lent Is Coming. Will Your Looks Survive?

Maybe it's not too late. Even during Lent, it's just a question of improving wardrobe and hair after all. Maybe if I added daily Mass to my Lenten devotions, I'd have a reason to do my hair more than once a week. And I could always try altering some of my thrift-shop treasures on my new second-hand sewing machine.

∞

Family Vacations (and Other Ways to Punish Your Kids)

Before Greg and I got married, I made him sign a prenuptial agreement that he would never invite, bring, or force me on a car trip that took longer than a day. (A day here is defined as the interval between sunrise and sunset.) Furthermore, he would never be complicit in such an invitation from another party.

Extreme? I've seen a lot of this great country of ours, most of it flashing by from the crowded backseat of my parents' family sedan.

The car was a dark-green Ford with black upholstery. The year, sometime in the Seventies. My parents thought it would be fun to drive their three youngest children to Missouri — from upstate New York, over a thousand miles — in the middle of summer with no air conditioning. My brother, sister, and I were too young to be taken seriously as conscientious objectors.

It was war, after all.

You all know how kids usually fight over who gets the window seats? Not the case here. The car was a two-door. Our parents controlled the windows. Perhaps they were punishing us because it was boil or get blown apart the whole way. Do not think, however, that in the absence of windows we had nothing to fight about.

Please Don't Drink the Holy Water!

When faced with the prospect of starting out at an indecent hour — three a.m. the first day — and driving until supper, all you can hope to do is find a place where you can sleep some of it off. We had turf wars over the floor, the seat, and the ledge above the backseat. I was the youngest — guess what I got? The reason given was that my body, when curled over the hump that ran across the middle of the floor, absorbed bumps the best. But we who were once younger siblings know the real reason. (You older siblings do, too, but I doubt whether you are losing any sleep over it. Fine, don't let it concern you. I would just like to be there when you get yours on Judgment Day.) By the end of the day, I was high on the noxious fumes. I whined. My mother told me to be quiet for heaven's sake. My sister offered to stick my head out the window at sixty mph.

My brother, the second youngest, got the ledge above the back seat. He got a sunburn, a fever, a headache, and maternal sympathy. My sister claimed squatter's rights over the seat for the duration. As she was armed and dangerous even while sleeping, my brother and I did not challenge her.

Still, there were times we bonded. For one thing, we were all threatened by "the Arm." Pop drove with his left and made sweeping backward and forward motions with his right whenever the noise got to be too much. Usually we heeded the Arm. But once a rush of giddiness brought on by fatigue overtook the three of us at the same time. We bounced all over the backseat and made faces at passing motorists. A heavily made-up blonde obliged and stuck her tongue out at us.

For amusement we played games. Alphabet Letters on Signs, Count the Volkswagens, and Cripple the Youngest. My sister had me bend my elbow, then rubbed it for a few minutes and told me to stick it, as such, out the window for five minutes. My reserves were so depleted that I suspected nothing. When I brought it back in, I couldn't unbend it. "You untie every one of those hairs!" my mom told my sister in exasperation.

The whole experience had its upside, though. It used up at least a half-hour.

Rest stops were a blessing. We went to the bathroom — a privilege, as the adage goes, rendered more dear from much anticipation. Then we hit the vending machines so as to appreciate the next rest stop all the better. After that, our parents paid us to go spend time in the gift shop. There we discovered all manner of items to delight the heart of a child. How we loved the plastic barf. It came with a picture of a lady saying, "Oops!" Back inside the car, it held our interest for at least fifteen miles. We talked about how we'd use it on our friends when we got home. But for some unexplained reason, when we returned, we could never find it. Our friends all thought we were making it up to impress them.

At the close of the day, Mom would read to Pop from the hotel/motel directory. There were three absolutes: affordability, cable, and a pool. The latter two were more important than beds. The pool was a sort of baptism, a way for the three of us to thrash all the evil out. Cable was a sedative before bedtime.

Finally, at the end of five days, our destination! A quiet household featuring my parents' best friends from two decades before, and their daughter — my sister's age. (*O God, why dost Thou maketh the wicked to prosper?*) This was the first time in our lives my brother and I looked good to each other.

We had two weeks of such fun and then the return trip to look forward to.

The trip was such a resounding success that the following year my parents took the three of us to North Dakota. Thirteen hundred miles.

Please Don't Drink the Holy Water!

So, you see, I was not going to extremes with the prenuptial agreement. Our children have no idea what they've been spared. This is the first time I am really able to talk about it.

My parents' other vacation of choice was camping. Now, I admit camping can be fun. We had some great times up in Maine at a camp that had toilets and showers. However, we often camped on our own tract of land in upstate New York, nestled on the shores of Lake Untamed Wilderness. The nearest intelligent life was Bigfoot. Our tent fit all ten of us. The roof was also generous — it took in water. Permeating this cozy atmosphere was the smell of damp cots and musty sleeping bags, not to mention surround-sound snoring.

All of this leads me to the present. Eight years ago, my husband started up an annual pilgrimage to the Shrine of the North American Martyrs in Auriesville, New York. It's modeled on the famous pilgrimage to Chartres, France, which, although a holy and ancient lineage, means four days of walking; camping; damp, musty sleeping bags and tents; and all-around rough-it conditions. My husband, kids, and many other families love it. It's a chance to be with other Catholics for a unique blend of prayer, penance, singing, jokes, fellowship, and really sore feet. If you don't mind subsisting on soup and granola, sleeping out of doors, and seeing your kids spattered with dust and mud, it's a wonderful time. At least that's what people tell me. It has been my consistent practice to arrive just in time to tend my family's wounds, nurse them back to health, and sleep in a house. This has worked beautifully for many years. Yet recently Greg hinted that it would be nice to have me there for the whole thing. Knowing how vocal I am when uncomfortable, I can only suppose that he wants to increase his penance level.

Unfortunately, I have no prenuptial agreement to fall back on. But this is not a problem, because I can prove that my reasons for not going are purely spiritual. First: the fact that Greg is the coordinator, and people will think me an unsupportive wife if I do not go, means seeking human respect and therefore pride. Second: anyone can see that pride is the wrong motivation to go on pilgrimage. It's a clear-cut case of the near occasion of sin. Third: we have always been taught that willingly to put oneself in the near occasion of sin is a sin. Therefore, for me to go on this pilgrimage would be a sin.

At this point Greg tells me that I missed my calling. I should have been a lawyer. Still, he is unconvinced. He says that pride need not be considered at all. The purpose of this pilgrimage is to make reparation to God. That it is moreover good for soul and body to sacrifice. And wouldn't it be meaningful if we all made the pilgrimage together as a family? I'll admit once or twice this has almost caused me to reconsider.

Maybe if I had a Winnebago.

∞

Grim and Grimy Fairy Tales

The Bedtime Story. It's got a reputation as glossy as Currier and Ives. Can't you see Mother bending to kiss the rosy cheek of her blond, curly-haired child? "Sweet dreams," she murmurs through delicate blushing lips, as the child snuggles down beneath the covers.

You'd never know that some of those fairy tales have skeletons in the closet. Literally.

Did you ever read the old, Germanic "fairy tales"? If so, you know that these may sport the same names as the modern cartoon versions, but what's inside is a totally different species. They are not the product of a pop culture trying to ingratiate itself with kids for the purpose of making money. They are the product of a post-Calvin Europe where fate rules, the guilty are damned, and decent behavior is a sign of predestination.

In one of the tales, an envious girl gets deservedly killed in place of her beautiful stepsister. As if that weren't lesson enough, drops of her blood call out eerily to the derangement of her evil, plotting mother. Then there is good old Cinderella. Her stepsisters are way beyond ugly and cranky; they're so ambitious, they cut off portions of their feet to fit into the glass slipper. Snow White's stepmother falls victim to her own black magic when it turns on her, causing her to dance herself to a burning grave. And, sorry to disappoint all you "Little Mermaid" fans. She doesn't get her prince at all. He forgets her and marries a proper, decent human girl. The poor mermaid dies of a broken heart.

Clearly this is not the stuff that sells. Who would buy Little Mermaid costumes under those circumstances? Even in today's violent society, I can't imagine finding toys that bleed or come with detachable body parts in my child's Yippie Meal.

This is not the sort of stuff with which you tuck in the wide-eyed and innocent — unless, of course, your aim is to bring on nightmares.

Now we're getting to the point. These fairy tales come from the days when it was a parents' world. If you wanted good behavior out of your kids, start them off young with the one about the nasty self-ish girl who trod on a loaf and ended up the underground prisoner of a witch. That'll teach 'em.

As a parent living in what has become a children's world, I see something to this. The formula is to identify a person's fears and link it to an undesirable behavior. After all, it works with dogs. Fear: being locked up in a dark garage all day. Undesirable behavior: eating upholstery. Connection. Good dog.

This was also the system of choice in America up to the early twentieth century. As a homeschooler, I discovered this when a friend gave me a complete set of nineteenth-century McGrim's Readers.

The boy in the following excerpt is eight.

The Devil's Brew

Look now at that sick boy. He is not sick for want of food. He drank whiskey. See how his face is pale and sad! He cannot run, nor jump, nor play. I hope you will not act like this boy. He is now a perfect idiot. He will probably die.

And this is just the Primary Reader.

People blame a lot of things for the loss of moral values among our young people. If you ask me, a return to the tried-and-true methods of scaring the evil out of kids is a long time coming.

We have no upholstery-chewers here, nor pint-size whiskey drinkers. But wherever there are children, there are undesirable behaviors. Our particular trouble was an overflowing toilet. I tried lecture after lecture, but got no results. Then, in a moment of desperation I turned to the bedtime horror story.

The Sad Little Toilet

Once upon a time there was a toilet. It was an only toilet. It had no brothers and sisters. But it was never lonely because it lived in a household of six-plus people. The "plus" was not old enough to use the toilet in the usual way, but she made up for it by visiting it often to play in it.

The toilet lived a busy, productive life. It had only one complaint. The children constantly forced it to eat too much toilet paper. Finally one day the toilet choked. One too many wads went in, and flush, bjoing, and pssh, pssh, pssh. Water came splashing back out.

Here, the kids frown and look concerned.

Pssh, pssh, pssh! The water flowed out from all directions, all over the bathroom floor and into the surrounding rooms. There seemed to be no stopping it.

Their eyes are as big as full moons. I continue:

"Are you sure you want to hear the scary end?"

They nod.

. . . It was not just water.

"Gross, Mom!"

The sad little toilet almost died that day, except for a brave youngster. Mom said someone had to reach down into the falls and turn off the lever at the bottom . . . and Daddy wasn't home!

The kids had to spend two hours cleaning it up.

"Aarah!"

Kids are writhing on the bed, choking, gasping for breath, as they imagine themselves drowning in toilet water. It is time for my Rod Serling imitation:

You may think you're safe, that it can't happen to you. That is what the family in our story thought. But sooner or later, when you least expect it, perhaps some night when you're all alone in the house . . . beware!

The End.

Tuck them in, kiss them goodnight, and hope nightmares do the rest.

Next up in the series, "How Smart Mouth Was Struck Dumb," followed by "The Tale of Clutter Quicksand."

Someday, these are going to be classics.

∞

There's No Place Like Home

In the Real World you don't often find the finest academics, the finest moral standards, the finest student body, and the finest teachers all under one roof. True, you don't find that in home schools either. What you do find is a dedicated teacher who loves each of the students as her own, and who wants them to be prepared not just for this life but the next.

This is why my husband tells me he feels so confident when he walks out the door in the morning. He knows the kids are with someone he can trust.

That is, until the day when I told them about circumcision. I don't know what got into me. We were reading the Bible like good little homeschoolers, and well, somebody asked.

Now, I have always been of the opinion that less is more. Here I refer to information. In delicate matters, I tend to make my answer as precise, academic, and diverting as possible.

So when one of the kids asked what circumcision was, you would think that I would have said something like, "A sign of initiation into the Old Covenant, the precursor of Baptism in the New." And indeed that is all I meant to say. I was tired. Where most people's conversation slows down until it comes to a halt when they're tired, mine speeds up until it crashes into something. As I recall, I started off all right, but by the time I was done, the kids had a list of questions (starting with, but not limited to, "Where is it?") for which I could not think of an answer. At least not one that met all three criteria of precise, academic, and diverting. Instead I did one of these, "My, isn't it getting late!" copouts.

When my husband came home that night, I confessed all.

He froze. His mouth hung open; he stopped breathing; he gaped; he almost drooled. He had the look of one who says, "Until this moment, I never really knew you."

We've been married over fifteen years. He should have known I was capable of such things. I have never hidden anything from him. As a cradle Catholic, I have an inner force that drives me to tell on myself at every opportunity, namely:

Guilt

Never underestimate the power of guilt. Many words have been written on the subject. Of all the evils modernity has put its energy into eradicating, guilt has proven stronger than bad breath. You realize this when you kneel in the confessional and whisper close enough to the priest's face that you know he can tell what you had for lunch. (The real reason they prefer to let you talk into their ear.) You don't care how embarrassing the combination of your lunch and your sins is; you have guilt, and you want to get rid of it.

What the Real World fails to grasp is that guilt is a gift from God. Indeed, how many of us Catholics really appreciate it? Estimates say about one in a hundred. (I got that by comparing the number of sinners in line for Confession on Saturday afternoon with the number in line for Communion on Sunday.)

Now, I am one of those people who guards my guilt jealously. In the first place, scrupulosity gallops in my family. I was born to

Catholic parents who educated me to have graphic ideas about hell rather than sex. At a tender age they sent me to the O.H.P.S. nuns[2] who took charge of my formal instruction. Yet, in spite of what people out in the Real World might presume, I count myself among the lucky.

I feel almost snobbish about guilt. I am part of a vast, ancient organization that ranks as the leading expert on it. The Church has long recognized its primeval motivating power. She has decided that, like other primeval motivators (lust shall be nameless), guilt can be channeled and, when applied correctly, is actually quite good for the soul.

For instance, after a day chasing the dog tail of perfection, Catholics are supposed to lie awake and examine their consciences. People think that this leads to neurosis. But I will warrant that there are billions of people who lie awake at night and examine their consciences, but don't realize that that is what they are doing. They feel terrible about it because no one has ever enlightened them that criticizing what they've said and done at the end of the day is a positive exercise. There is no self-esteem built into their guilt that would cause them to say, "There. I failed again. God loves me more for admitting it. In the morning I will do something about it. Now I can sleep in Elysium." Catholics go to Confession. Other people buy Nyquil.

Catholic homeschool mothers are even more prone to guilt than other Catholics. Often, guilt is the reason they decide to homeschool in the first place. After all, they really should be doing the utmost for their kids. Their kids might get corrupted in the Real World, and it would be their fault if they could have prevented it. Once homeschooling is begun, however, the guilt does

[2] Order of Hair-Pulling Sisters.

not subside. It swings the other way. Was this the right decision? Are they doing all they can? Are the kids missing out? So they run their kids to all sorts of extracurricular activities. Then they turn around again and worry that they are letting the world in through the back door.

Now, I've been around my share of Protestant homeschoolers too. But none of them has dared to get close enough for me to ask them why they are always so cheerful. So I asked a convert who also happens to be a priest. His words: "It was just great. We were saved!" So that's it. Protestants live every day with the conviction that they are going to live one day in heaven with the Protestant Lord who is kind and merciful, slow to anger, and rich. The Catholic Lord, on the other hand, is coming to judge the living and the dead. No one is exempt — not even Catholic homeschooling mothers with ten kids. Yet, no matter what a Protestant has done, even if it merits beating his breast and crying on national TV that he has "sinned," he can't go to hell.

Is this fair? Is this logical? Is this interesting?

Without hell, guilt, and sin, why bother to homeschool?

As a refugee from the Real World, I am an expert in the above three. I am eminently qualified to fulfill my husband's mandate of homeschooling: to shelter our children from the evils of the Real World while young, and to prepare them to enter it later with solid Catholic consciences.

Unfortunately, I brought a lot of baggage with me from the old country — some of it much worse than telling the kids the real reason the Israelites were lousy evangelists.

Slang

Chief of which is: *duh*. I was unconscious of this until my husband came home from work and wanted to know where the kids picked up that kind of talk, and they said, "Mom." This became a real problem when we met the bishop. We were in a large party at his residence with our fourth child, golden-haired and then age two. Bishopbait. We were not surprised that he singled us out. At that time, she was just learning her name and often mixed it up with her age. So when he said, "Hello, dear, what's your name?" she said, "Two." He didn't get it. "What's that you say, dear?" "Two!" she said again. "What is it?" he said one final time. She looked at him in exasperation and said, "Two, *duh!*" Greg and I looked at each other, our hearts united in silent prayer. It worked. He turned to us. "What's that she said? Two dogs?" We nodded, wondering if it counted as lying.

Cousin to slang is the adolescent insult line, such as, "Does your face hurt? It's killing me." Now, I do not wish to give the wrong impression. I do not talk to my children this way directly. I tell them about these things so that they will not be ignorant of what is happening in the Real World. It is a deterrent, like Drug-ed in public schools or what was once found in every Catholic school, Hell-ed. As the girls get older and go out more, Insult-ed becomes necessary.

Suppose they are caught in an exchange that begins, "You're ugly." What's the proper response?

A. Tears?
B. Dashing out to buy cosmetics?
C. "Oh yeah? So's your *face*"?
D. "Yeah, you wish"?

You and I both know that choice C is correct. We are adults after all.

Without Insult-ed, there is the very real danger that a child will choose A or B. Choice D opens the insultee up for a second insult like, "Were your parents first cousins?"

Please Don't Drink the Holy Water!

Youthful Exploits

Yes, I have a past. Some of it is not my fault. I was born with the ability to burp on demand. My parents were ashamed, but my friends admired it. While they were attempting to swallow air I had already added names, such as Ralph, to my repertoire.

Now, I never deliberately told our kids about this gift until they discovered they had it, too. Knowing how quickly these things get out of hand, it was up to me to provide a positive mentoring experience.

When I was a teen, I became famous for "Hawaiian nose hums." I was in a class by myself. Nobody I knew could even come close. For those who do not know what I am referring to, try this exercise. Think of the tune that goes: "*Aloha oi. . . .* " Then place your forefinger on one side of your nose, and begin humming. Stroke the nostril for each note. Got it? I bet you still can't beat me at it.

These exploits, although tame enough in their way, somehow come across as far worse than any exploits that the kids' peers could possibly do. This is because they were done by me and so tarnish the maternal image: the image that I was born with a basket of laundry in one hand and an academic planner book in the other.

Disasters in the News

Who would want their kids to watch the L.A. riots, O.J.'s high-speed chase, or the burning of Waco? Not I. For this reason we've always sheltered our kids from television news. Then one day, probably during history, it occurred to me that our kids really should know about current events. So I described some of these things in detail, drew out the political ramifications, and left the kids to draw their own conclusions about the deplorable condition of the Real World. After the lesson, they ran off to start a novena.

"You've been teaching current events again, haven't you?"

The Liturgical Surprises of My Youth

Greg and I have taken great care over the sorts of liturgies we bring our children to. We refuse to subject them to the liturgical instability that was so common in our young lives, it was almost predictable.

Please Don't Drink the Holy Water!

But the question sometimes nags me: What if, one day in their adult life, they innocently wander into a place like St. Opprobrius — the parish of my youth? I felt I simply must share with them my own experiences. How Bob Dylan edged out Fr. Faber in the missalette, and the grape-juice/love-loaf Mass in our school cafeteria. Then there was the time our parochial-school class went to First Friday and the priest said something objectionable that went completely over the heads of the entire class and which I do not even now recall. All I remember is that my mother, who was in the back of the church, suddenly materialized, spoke briefly to the teacher and then ushered me out of the church. (In the last case, Mom was the surprise.) I must reiterate that I do not set out intending to tell the kids these things. I am only dangerous in moments of fatigue. At least they now know what they've been spared and are in a better position to appreciate the choices their father and I have made. We give them only positive experiences of the priesthood and religious life. They have met numerous priests and nuns who are shining examples of their vocations. People whom it is impossible to imagine ever humming a nose in their lives.

In the end, I have to agree that there is no place like home. I remain the only bad influence in our children's lives.

∞

The Golden Years

Scene: A recurring dream. The year is 2066. I am one hundred years old. I am in my seventy-fifth consecutive year of homeschooling.

I am at the bank on a Friday morning with five children ages two through thirteen. Teller hands out five lollipops and says, "Don't you have school today?" to Child Four, youngest of the articulate type. Sinister of her — trying to buy information from a six-year-old with a penny sucker. Not to mention cheap.

Child Four (looks up at me and shrugs): Um, I don't know.
Instantly a chorus erupts:
Child One: We don't go to school.
Child Two: Don't say that. We do too. We're homeschooled.
Child Three: Except we don't have to take a bus from the bedroom to the kitchen. Ha, ha.
Child One: We're on lunch. Is that right, Mom? Or are we just taking the rest of the day off again?
Chorus: Please, please! Oh pretty please!
Child Two: That's not fair. I did math in the car.
Child Three: We could count this as a field trip. We go on a lot of field trips.

Please Don't Drink the Holy Water!

Teller frowns slightly.

Me: Would you believe it's a snow day?

Teller glances out the window. May.

Me: What I mean is, we still have three snow days to make up. After all, we must keep up with state standards.

Teller: I was just wondering one thing. What are you planning to do when someday your children go out into the Real World?

Me: How many times have you been in this dream, lady? Haven't you figured out that this is never going to end? This is the past, the present, the future! These kids are never going to grow up. I'm trapped in homeschool Jumangi. With every turn, we get deeper into workbooks, extracurricular activities, and pregnancy. My husband and I will never retire. We'll never have a second honeymoon in our golden years. And you know what? It's all your fault. All these years I hand over a wad of cash, and you never give me a lollipop. Maybe if just once you gave me one, it would break the spell.

Child One: Want a lick of mine?

Child Two: I haven't finished mine yet. You can have the rest, Mom.

Child Three: Take mine! I was saving it for you. I didn't really want it anyway. It's only half-licked.

Child Four hands me a wet stick.

Child Five: Crunch.

Teller (smiles at the kids, pulls out her stash, and holds a lollipop out to me): You've earned it.

But suddenly I don't want it. In fact, everything I thought I wanted I would now trade for five wet lollipop sticks.

Me: No, thanks. I don't want out of this dream after all. I don't want to wake up and find that my kids are grown, and that my job is done. What I've got *is* the Real World.

The Golden Years

I pick up my toddler, extend a second hand to our six-year-old, and with a third beckon the other kids to follow. We all leave for home.

These are the golden years.

Susie Lloyd

Susie Lloyd was born into a large Catholic family that spanned the baby-boom, hippie, and preppie decades, and was educated in public and parochial schools and in a parent-run catechetical center. She's a Catholic Press Association award winner and frequent contributor to a variety of Catholic magazines. She holds a B.A. from Thomas More College of Liberal Arts in Merrimack, New Hampshire and an M.O.M. degree from her husband, Greg, and her five homeschooled daughters. Her sixth child is due in January 2005.

Sophia Institute Press®

Sophia Institute® is a nonprofit institution that seeks to restore man's knowledge of eternal truth, including man's knowledge of his own nature, his relation to other persons, and his relation to God. Sophia Institute Press® serves this end in numerous ways: it publishes translations of foreign works to make them accessible to English-speaking readers; it brings out-of-print books back into print; and it publishes important new books that fulfill the ideals of Sophia Institute®. These books afford readers a rich source of the enduring wisdom of mankind.

Sophia Institute Press® makes these high-quality books available to the general public by using advanced technology and by soliciting donations to subsidize its general publishing costs. Your generosity can help Sophia Institute Press® to provide the public with editions of works containing the enduring wisdom of the ages. Please send your tax-deductible contribution to the address below.

For your free catalog, call:
Toll-free: 1-800-888-9344

Sophia Institute Press® ✦ Box 5284 ✦ Manchester, NH 03108
www.sophiainstitute.com

Sophia Institute® is a tax-exempt institution as defined by the
Internal Revenue Code, Section 501(c)(3). Tax I.D. 22-2548708.